A SURVIVOR'S GUIDE TO BORDERLINE
PERSONALITY DISORDER

The Borderline Blueprint

CHARTING THE COURSE THROUGH THE EMOTIONAL TIDES OF BPD

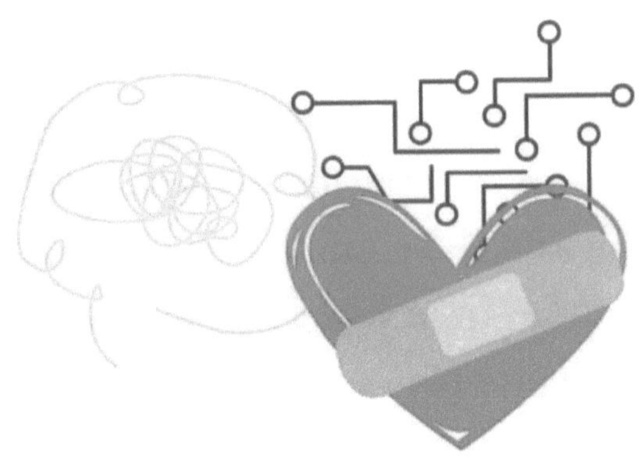

KUNJAN SHARMA

Title: The Borderline Blueprint

Author: Kunjan Sharma

ABOUT THE AUTHOR

Kunjan Sharma has dedicated years to researching mental health, particularly borderline personality disorder (BPD). Her deep personal interest in psychiatry, combined with extensive study and firsthand experiences, led her to write The Borderline Blueprint. Through this book, she aims to bridge the gap between clinical knowledge and real-life struggles, offering insights that are both research-backed and deeply empathetic.

For inquiries or permissions, contact:

Kunjan21098@gmail.com

Published by:

First Edition: March, 2025

Printed in India

DISCLAIMER

This book is based on personal experiences with Borderline Personality Disorder (BPD), healing, and self-discovery. I am not a medical professional, therapist, or psychologist. The content shared here is intended for informational and personal reflection purposes only. **Do not use the content of book to self-diagnose.** BPD manifests differently in each individual, and what has worked for me may not be suitable for everyone.If you are struggling with your mental health, **I strongly encourage seeking professional guidance from a licensed therapist or psychiatrist.**

Additionally, this book may discuss **sensitive topics**, including trauma, **suicide,** emotional distress, **sexual abuse** and **self-destructive behaviors.** Please read with caution and prioritize your well-being. If you are in crisis, reach out to a trusted professional or a crisis helpline in your area.

By reading this book, you acknowledge that the information provided is **not a substitute for professional medical or psychological advice.** The **author and publisher are not responsible** for any decisions made based **on the content of this book.**

Your healing journey is unique—take what resonates and leave what doesn't. Be kind to yourself.

Preface

"It is the Matter of Time and the Chemistry of Brain"

The Borderline Blueprint, delve into the raw and unfiltered world of living with Borderline Personality Disorder (BPD). Written from the deeply personal perspective of someone navigating this complex condition. This book offers a unique blend of lived experience, insight, and practical guidance. Making this Complex Disorder easy to understand by everyone.

Through real life incidences, thoughtful reflections, and actionable strategies, The Borderline Blueprint provides readers with a comprehensive guide to understanding the person living with BPD. Whether you're someone living with the condition, a loved one seeking insight, this book is an invaluable resource for navigating the complexities of BPD with empathy, courage, and hope.

Join the journey of self-discovery, healing, and empowerment, and uncover the blueprint to a life redefined beyond the borderline

TABLE OF CONTENTS

CHAPTER ONE

IN THE GRIP OF CHAOS

The night was Cold with silence haunting her, oppressive and dark, like a weight pressing down on her chest. It felt like she was sinking, swallowed by shadows she could never outrun. **Jane** lay curled on her bed with teary-eyes and a mental discomfort she was unaware of. Each day was agonizing than the last and she felt each one down to the bone? This unbearable pain gnawed at her, relentless of hunger, leaving behind a raw, throbbing emptiness. She was clueless , wasn't able to think anything clearly- mentally disorganized , mind seems foggy, just crying for hours from evening to next morning but irony was still don't know the reason. She became a baby in pain unable to explain but crying hard for help.

Days blurred into nights and nights into the hollow echoes of silence. It was a silence that wasn't calm or peaceful but heavy in tons maybe or more.

Jane always longed for love, care, and attention—a desire that took root in her childhood. Her parents were deeply caring but often occupied with their jobs, striving to provide a life free from the financial struggles they had endured. Having experienced hardship themselves, they were determined to ensure Jane and her brother, **Josh**, would never have to face the same difficulties.

Family—the one place she believed would understand her when the rest of the world didn't. She trusted that they would see her pain, that they would know her heart, when words failed. And they tried, with all the love and knowledge they had. But no matter how much they cared, they couldn't truly grasp the depth of her struggles.

She felt a profound disappointment, a sense of abandonment that cut deeper because it came from those she held closest. She tried to show them her reality, to make them feel the weight of what she was carrying, and she begged for help. They gave their all, pouring their efforts into supporting her. But despite their love and best intentions, they couldn't reach the place within her that needed healing the most.

Despite their parent's best efforts, life wasn't easy for either Jane or Josh. Josh battled with drugs and mental health issues, adding to the weight both siblings carried. Yet, in the eyes of society, it was their parents who garnered the most sympathy—seen as victims of their children's troubles. Few paused to acknowledge the pain and struggles Jane and Josh endured, leaving them isolated in their suffering.

Jane cared deeply for Josh and felt his pain every time others spoke harshly about him. She understood his struggles in a way few did. All Josh ever wanted was the love and acceptance of his family. However, over time, he began to feel unwanted, as though he was a constant source of disappointment—someone who caused trouble and tarnished their parents' reputation in the eyes of society. This rejection, especially from the family he once cherished, bred resentment, particularly toward his mother, whom he had loved him the most. Yet beneath the resentment, he still longed for their love and understanding.

In his search for acceptance, Josh sought love outside the home and found solace in a girl who made him believe in love again. But when she left him for someone else, he couldn't let go. He clung to her, convinced that no one else would ever love him. What Josh didn't realize was that it wasn't her he loved, but the idealized version of her he had created in his mind—the hope she represented in his desperate need for love and belonging.

Both Jane and Josh were trapped in their own battles, yet their struggles took different forms. Jane, though burdened by her pain, was aware of her emotions, able to express them, and determined to find a way forward. Josh, however, was consumed by a relentless darkness. Unable to articulate his feelings, he masked his pain with anger and harshness, lashing out at those around him.

Despite her own hardships, Jane could sense the depth of Josh's suffering. She reached out to him time and again, trying to understand and help. But each time, he pushed her away, his pain too overwhelming to allow anyone in. Lost in his torment, Josh turned to drugs as his only escape. For Jane, this became a new nightmare—haunted by the fear that one day, she might lose him forever. The thought of his life slipping away felt like an unbearable ending, one she never wanted to face.

Jane longed for both her and Josh to break free from the weight they had carried for years. Josh, though younger, had been battling this darkness for nearly eight years, while Jane had endured her own struggles for six. What made it even more painful was the constant fight within themselves just to keep going, only to face yet another battle each day—seeking acceptance from their own family.

Jane sensed that something might be amiss with her thoughts or feelings, so she decided to seek professional guidance for clarity and support.

Then came the interventions, appointments with strangers who'd ask questions she barely had the strength to answer, probing into wounds she hadn't known were festering. The

Psychiatrist's place smelled clinical, with some of posters on depression, seeking professional help and paperwork. Their questions felt like a hollow repetition, questions they'd asked a hundred others. But Jane went through the motions. Nodded at prescriptions. Followed the instructions. She was diagnosed with borderline personality disorder and major depression—terms that felt like distant, incomprehensible labels to her at the time.

"Borderline personality disorder is a psychological disorder characterized by a pervasive pattern of instability in affect regulation, impulse control, interpersonal relationships, and self-image. Clinically people with BPD may have high health care utilization, health-sabotaging behaviors, chronic or vague somatic concerns, aggressive outbursts, high-risk sexual behaviors, and substance use. Borderline personality disorder is thought to be caused by a combination of genetic, neurobiologic, and psychosocial factors, with moderate evidence for genetic transmission and heritability, combined with environmental factors such as repeated trauma. Trauma and

neglect may exacerbate biologic predisposition and behavioral tendencies already present in those with borderline personality disorder".

Source: *Mendez-Miller M, Naccarato J, Radico JA. Borderline Personality Disorder. Am Fam Physician. 2022 Feb 1;105(2):156-161. PMID: 35166488.*

The medication was supposed to help, but soon it became a crutch. One pill became two, and on some nights, when the loneliness screamed too loudly, three. She thought it was a solution, but it was just another descent. She felt trapped between worlds: one dulled by the numbing fog of medication, the other a relentless storm of emotions. Sleep became an escape she couldn't control, a drug she craved to flee reality.

The world around slowed, blurring at the edges as you fixate on the narrowest points of pain and release. The first time she held that blade to her wrist, it was as if she was hovering outside herself, watching, silently pleading for someone, anyone, to see, to stop her, to understand but no one saw. It escalated to a point where it became increasingly difficult to manage and Self harm kicked it.

The sting of the blade, sharp and cold, felt strangely alive, each cut was fleeting moment where she wasn't numb. It left marks, little secrets only her skin would bear witness to. The cycle escalated, each moment harder than the last. Those pills the psychiatrist prescribed seems the easy solution in hand, firstly she hesitated then swallowed them handful and again. Minutes after vision got blurry and her movements faltered as if the world was slipping away. Everything seemed to be leaving her grasp, replaced by an overwhelming sense of deep, tranquil peace. Tears welled up in her eyes, her speech slurred and shaky. In that fragile moment, she called her mom, in trembling voice and said, **"I'm not okay."**

She slipped into unconsciousness and was rushed to the hospital, where reality blurred into haunting voices she couldn't distinguish from the reality. Unaware of she was hallucinating, she cried out in anguish, her voice was loud, raw and trembling with pain. Desperation consumed her as she begged to be left alone, resisting every attempt at care. Her frail body fought against the hands that tried to help, forcing them to restrain her trembling limbs, holding her down as she struggled, lost in a torment she couldn't escape.

But waking up was anything but calm. She came under harsh lights, the sterile smell of disinfectants filling the room. Her body ached, Nose was in immense pain, and a pipe was forced to take out the poison created by the medicine which was supposed to keep her alive. The worse was the cacophony of voices around her, harsh, condemning, each word driving deeper into her, like a barrage of needles piercing through the remnants of her resolve. They shouted things that carved more painfully than any blade could, branding Jane with their anger and disappointment.

"Weak", They shouted!

The word burned. It clung her to, sinking into her bones, reverberating until she could hear anything else. And there she lay, drenched in shame, stripped bare, feeling as she was no longer a person but a fragile shell of every hurt and flaw they saw in her.

Before healing could even begin, another wave would crash, dragging her deeper, into a place where even the idea of escape felt like an unreachable fantasy. And yet, in the most twisted of ways, the thought of release, of ending the pain, felt comforting. Suicide ideation slipped into her mind, offering solace in the darkness, whispering that maybe, just maybe, this was the way to find peace.

But even in that moment, there was a small part of her that fought back, a voice buried so deeply within the shadows that she could barely hear it. It reminded her that somewhere, beyond this agony, healing was still possible. And so, she held on, however fragile the grip, hoping that one day the darkness might lift.

But it was like trying to fill a canyon with handfuls of sand, her efforts slipping through her fingers. A consuming ache settled in her stomach, an ache that was somehow too deep for words and too dark for tears. She wondered if anyone else felt it—this black hole in the heart, this need for something she couldn't even name. The thought of it never being filled made her chest tighten with panic, each breath a battle.

Impulses clawed at her. Her skin felt foreign, like an armor too tight, suffocating her with its presence. The edge of pain promised clarity, if only for a moment. A line across her skin, a feeling she could control, might at least drown out the screaming silence.

And so, she floated in the space between despair and hope, numbness and agony, an endless limbo of feeling too much and not enough.

But then there was the fear—the fear of being alone, of being left behind, unwanted. The terror that no one could bear to stay, that every connection was a heartbeat away from slipping through her grasp. Her mind twisted the smallest glance, the faintest tone, into signs of inevitable abandonment. It was a self-fulfilling prophecy that left her pushing people away, then begging them to stay. The push and pull tore her apart, leaving her feeling empty and monstrous, unable to keep anyone close without hurting them or herself.

"Feelings of isolation and loneliness typically characterize individuals with borderline personality disorder and a history of trauma, as does their tendency to act out these un-mentalized experiences of the self. Trauma, and particularly attachment trauma, may undermine epistemic trust (i.e., the willingness and openness to consider new knowledge acquired by means of social communications as trustworthy, potentially personally relevant, and of generalizable significance to integrate into one's life). As a result, the traumatized individual may become completely cut off from social learning. Epistemic vigilance among traumatized individuals may also be accompanied by initial excessive epistemic credulity, often driven by strong wishes to be able to rely on a trusted other, rendering such individuals vulnerable to exploitation and abuse, which then further increases their epistemic vigilance".

STOLEN INNOCENCE

Jane was just five years old, a little girl whose world was simple and full of joy. Her days were a rhythm of school, play, and laughter, untouched by words like fear, betrayal, or trauma. Growing up in a close-knit village, she had never been warned not to trust anyone—because why would she? Everyone was family. She called neighbors "uncle" and "aunt," feeling safe in the warmth of her community.

Among them was an elderly man, her grandfather's friend, a kind-faced shopkeeper in his sixties. He was someone she liked—a familiar presence who always greeted her with a smile and pockets full of candies and biscuits. Whenever he got new snacks in his shop, he would offer them to her first. To Jane, he was generous, almost magical, always making her feel special.

Then came that Sunday.

He visited her home, speaking to her mother about a ritual that required her presence. Her mother, unsuspecting, agreed without hesitation. Jane, too, had no reason to question it. Why would she? This was someone she had known and trusted, someone who had only ever been kind.

Hand in hand, they walked through the village, past the familiar sights and sounds, until they reached his home.

The shutters of his shop were down—it was closed for the day. Inside, the house was unusually quiet. She looked around for his family but saw no one.

Still, she wasn't afraid. She was simply curious.

When he led her toward the godown, she followed without a second thought. She thought maybe he was about to show her something exciting—a new stock of chocolates, her favorite biscuits, something special just for her. After all, that's what always happened before.

But this time, something felt different.

And Jane, in all her innocence, had no idea that this time would change everything.

Even now, She remember that room vividly, every detail frozen in my mind as if no time has passed. There was a large wooden table in the center, worn with age, where he sat and motioned for her to come closer. Without hesitation, She did.

He lifted her onto his lap, just as she had done many times before. To Jane, it was nothing unusual. Maybe he was going to ruffle her hair, tell her a story, or offer her another sweet treat—things that once felt so normal, so safe.

But then, something changed.

His hands moved in a way that felt different—wrong. A discomfort stirred within her, unfamiliar yet undeniable. Her small body tensed, but she didn't fully understand why. She only knew that, for the first time in her little world, something didn't feel safe anymore. He tried to take her pants off and started touching her inappropriately- which she couldn't understand but was uncomfortable.

All she wanted in that moment was to run—to escape that room, to be anywhere but there. Her tiny legs moved as fast as they could, carrying her toward the door, but when she reached there, she realized she was too small. Her fingers stretched desperately for the lock, but it was just out of reach. Panic swelled inside her.

Up until that point, he had been gentle.

Jane banged on the door with all the strength my little hands could muster, tears streaming down her face as I pleaded to be let out. But he didn't react. He just sat there, smoking, watching her without a word, as if her cries didn't exist.

And then, he moved.

Without hesitation, he grabbed her, dragging her back to the table as if her struggle meant nothing. His grip was firm, unshaken by her resistance. Jane was just a child— small, powerless against the force that held her.

He pinned her down with one hand as effortlessly as if he were holding a doll. The other held his cigarette, its smoke curling into the air and settling over her. Jane coughed, her sobs mixing with the thick, bitter air, but he didn't stop. He didn't hesitate.

And in that moment, for the first time in her life, she knew what fear truly was. A fear that would never leave her. He inserted his fingers and Jane cried in pain.

Jane's world changed in a moment she never saw coming. One evening, in the familiar safety of a neighbor's home, everything took a turn she couldn't have imagined.

What started as an ordinary visit ended in horror? A hand silenced her screams, a force held her down as she fought back, tears streaming down her face. But there was no mercy, no hesitation. When her struggle wasn't enough, the threat came—words meant to keep her silent forever. The burning pain seared into her skin, a reminder of the warning: Speak, and you'll suffer more. Tell anyone, and you'll destroy your family.

And then, as if nothing had happened, he shifted. The mask of familiarity returned—an elder figure offering snacks, pretending the moment before had never existed. But Jane knew. Her body knew.

She walked home in silence. No one was there. The house was empty, but so was she. She turned on the TV, finished her homework, moved through the motions of a normal day. But when night fell, she lay in bed, staring at the clock, hearing nothing but its ticking. Sleep didn't come. Instead, self-blame did. A cruel voice in her mind whispered that somehow, this was her fault. That night, her reflection in her own mind changed forever.

After few days again, he led her back to the dim, suffocating space where no one could hear her protest. This time, the violation went even further—force, humiliation, and a helplessness so consuming that it left an imprint on her very existence. The moment shattered something deep inside her, a wound that would never fully heal.

Her hatred for herself only grew. The weight of what had happened clung to her like an unbearable shadow.

That evening, she sat outside her school, staring at the sky as the minutes passed—7 p.m., then 8 p.m. Still, no one from home came looking for her. When she finally returned, her mother asked only if she had finished her homework. No questions about where she had been or why she was late. For the first time, Jane felt truly abandoned. A thought crept into her mind—Maybe she already knows. Maybe that's why she's distant. And from that moment, a pattern of misunderstanding took root, shaping the way she saw her world.

But it didn't end there. For three long years, it continued. Every time she tried to resist, the punishment followed—burns, cruelty, horrors that words could never fully capture. Three years of suffering in silence, with no one to save her.

It didn't stopped here and was getting worse every single day, reached to an extent where he forced himself on her and penetrated- and Her soul died for that moment.

Jane wasn't sure if her parents ever noticed the changes in her—the way she withdrew, the way she barely ate. They were absorbed in their own world, their own responsibilities. Whatever they sensed, they never asked.

It wasn't until she was 9 that she was sent to a boarding school. And there, something unexpected happened. Day by day, the weight of those memories began to fade, as if her mind was shielding her from them. By the time she reached 19 or 20, it was as though they had been erased.

But trauma never truly disappears—it lingers in the body, in the subconscious. And now, she feels every scar she once forgot. The constant fear of being watched. The panic at the thought of being touched. The deep, aching wounds of abandonment, self-hatred, and shattered trust.

She longed for a place that felt safe. Sometimes, that longing became overwhelming—leading her to overexpress, to seek comfort with blind trust, to attach too quickly. Her emotions no longer felt like her own; they were tied to others, dictated by their actions, their approval, and their presence.

This was the beginning of something she wouldn't understand until much later—the roots of a struggle she would carry for years. Which changed everything for her.

Jane was already battling severe anxiety, a burden that seemed to grow heavier with each passing day. Yet, she pushed herself relentlessly to stay on track with her college course, determined not to let her struggles define her. Amidst all this, a new challenge emerged—her teacher, Mrs. Morgan. Mrs. Morgan, known for her brilliance, was pregnant for the fourth time after enduring the heartbreak of three miscarriages. Her mental state was fragile, but her intellect remained sharp. Jane deeply respected her resilience and never responded when Mrs. Morgan's behavior turned harsh. But what began as subtle hostility soon escalated into relentless mental torment. Mrs. Morgan began treating Jane partially, for reasons only she maybe aware of.

The situation reached a breaking point one day when Jane, broken by the emotional abuse, collapsed in the laboratory she was working in. To cover her actions and avoid scrutiny, Mrs. Morgan spread the drug rumor, casting doubt on Jane's well-being. She spreading false rumors that Jane was using drugs and is mentally unstable.

Jane, unaware of the malicious gossip, was taken home after the incident, unable to speak for three days due to the mental block caused by the trauma. A month later, when she returned to college, everything felt different. The atmosphere was tense, and people acted distant. Confused, she asked her hostel roommate what had changed. That's when she learned about the rumors. The lies had taken root, isolating her even further. Confronting the situation felt impossible. Her anxiety worsened, and her medication doses were increased, leaving her numb and voiceless on the outside while, inside, she was breaking—silently enduring the weight of everything that had happened.

Devastated after learning about the rumors, Jane broke down and called her mother, pleading to leave college. But her parents, unaware of the depth of her suffering, urged her to endure just a little longer-reminding her that it was the final semester. Disheartened and feeling unheard, Jane stayed, withdrawing from her family. The weight of the rumors and the inability to confront Mrs. Morgan consumed her thoughts.

Mrs. Morgan, sensing Jane's silence, grew more confident in her cruelty. Jane's anxiety spiraled daily, reaching unbearable levels. One day, she nearly collapsed again. A concerned student reported it to Mrs. Morgan, who dismissed it as "another drama" and sent Jane back to the hostel.

On her way, Jane stopped at the college dispensary, desperate for help. Tearful and panicked, she begged for assistance, but instead of calming her, the doctor fed into the rumors. He questioned her about her family: "Are your parents separated? Why does only your mother pick you up, never your father?"

The questions stung like salt on an open wound. Overwhelmed by the insensitivity, Jane slammed her hand on the table and stormed out, tears streaming down her face. She returned to her hostel, locked herself in her room, and in a state of utter despair, began taking her medication one pill after another-desperately trying to numb the pain. The overdose left her unconscious, plunging her into a darkness far deeper than she had ever known.

That day, Jane made a life-altering decision—she would quit her medication and treatment. She believed the very things meant to help her had made her vulnerable, leaving her exposed to people like Mrs. Morgan who took advantage of her struggles. But this decision came with a new challenge, surviving without the medications she had relied on daily for the past five years.

Without the support of her medication, her mental and physical health deteriorated rapidly. The pressure became too much, and soon she was hospitalized again, caught in the same vicious cycle of breaking down, receiving treatment, and returning home—only for the struggle to begin anew.

In an attempt to protect its reputation, the college issued a letter stating that Jane's health required her to complete her remaining coursework from home and sit for her exams remotely. However, even at home, the battle wasn't over. Her family, though concerned, struggled to understand the depth of her pain. Each day brought new challenges, and Jane found herself fighting a different battle—alone, misunderstood, and still searching for peace amidst the chaos.

Individuals with borderline personality disorder have an underlying vulnerability to emotional hyperarousal states and social and interpersonal stressors. Evidently from various studies nearly one-third of patients with borderline personality disorder have been raped or sexually assaulted in course of time.

Courage was her refusal to surrender, even after countless failed attempts. It was in those moments when the world felt heavy, and hope seemed distant, that she stood tall, summoning every ounce of strength from the fragments left within her. She never accepted the failure and perceptions thrown her way; she fought back relentlessly. Her journey was marked by endless bad days, sleepless nights, tears, frustrations, crushing disappointments, abandonment, and deep mental scars.

Yet, amidst it all, she began to care for herself, Started with one small step at a time. Some days, just eating a meal felt like an insurmountable task. Another day, managing to get out of bed. Then, on the third day, she would feel though she had lost all progress, standing at zero once again. But she refused to give in and turned the fourth day into a new day one, starting over with unwavering determination. Every setback became a chance to rebuild, and through it all, she taught herself how to keep moving forward.

She struggled with her weight, carrying some extra kilograms beyond her ideal, and her body image left her feeling deeply insecure. The reflection in the mirror often stole her confidence, and the voices around her only made it worse. People told her she wasn't good enough, that she lacked consistency, that she couldn't stick to anything— whether it was her work or her goals.

But she refused to let those words define her. Determined to feel confident in her own skin, she started eating healthier and working out, not just to change her appearance but to reclaim her sense of self. She made a promise to herself to show up, to go to work every single day, no matter how heavy her doubts felt.

Slowly, she crafted her own ways to cope, turning those criticisms into fuel for her resilience. It wasn't easy, but with every small step, she began to rebuild the confidence that others had tried to take away.

It all began with an impulsive decision to get a puppy—a choice that many doubted she could handle. But what started as a whim quickly became one of the most transformative experiences of her life. That little puppy became her world, and for the first time, she felt a profound sense of responsibility, almost like a mother caring for her child.

This tiny life brought a shift in her. She became active, stepping out of her comfort zone, and found herself motivated to care for him, often forgetting her own pain in the process. She nurtured him with immense love, pouring her heart into every little moment. While everyone around her believed she would give up within days, she proved them all wrong.

Even now, that dog is her greatest source of happiness, waking her up each morning with unconditional love and reminding her that life is still beautiful. He showed her that there will always be someone who loves you just as you are—without complaints, judgment, or criticism. By taking responsibility for her choice, she unknowingly chose to heal herself. Through him, she found strength, purpose, and the courage to embrace life again.

This daily struggle left their wounds deeper and their frustrations heavier. Yet, despite the relentless pain and overwhelming trauma, Jane and Josh continued to push forward. They clung to the fragile hope that, one day, they would make it through this vast ocean of darkness, pain, and struggle—believing that somewhere ahead, light and peace awaited them.

CHAPTER TWO

DECODING BORDERLINE PERSONALITY DISORDER: UNDERSTANDING THE SCIENCE.

BORDERLINE PERSONALITY DISORDER

Diagnostic criteria according to **DSM 5 TR** <u>(Diagnostic and Statistical Manual of Mental disorders)</u>

A pervasive pattern of instability of interpersonal relationships, self-image, and affects, and marked impulsivity, beginning by early adulthood and present in a variety of contexts, as indicated by **five (or more)** of the following:

1. Frantic efforts to avoid real or imagined abandonment. (Note: Do not include suicidal or self-mutilating behavior covered in Criterion 5.)

2. A pattern of unstable and intense interpersonal relationships characterized by alternating between extremes of idealization and devaluation.

3. Identity disturbance: markedly and persistently unstable self-image or sense of self.

4. Impulsivity in at least two areas that are potentially self-damaging (e.g., spending, sex, substance abuse, reckless driving, binge eating). (Note: Do not include suicidal or self-mutilating behavior covered in Criterion 5.)

5. Recurrent suicidal behavior, gestures, or threats, or self-mutilating behavior.

6. Affective instability due to a marked reactivity of mood (e.g., intense episodic dysphoria, irritability, or anxiety usually lasting a few hours and only rarely more than a few days).

7. Chronic feelings of emptiness.

8. Inappropriate, intense anger or difficulty controlling anger (e.g., frequent displays of temper, constant anger, recurrent physical fights).

9. Transient, stress-related paranoid ideation or severe dissociative symptoms.

---

1. FRANTIC EFFORTS TO AVOID REAL OR IMAGINED ABANDONMENT.

Individuals with BPD often experience an intense fear of being abandoned, whether the threat is real or imagined.

This fear can manifest as **desperate attempts to prevent separation or rejection.** They might go to great lengths to keep someone close, such as constantly seeking reassurance, making excessive phone calls, or even pleading with others not to leave.

<u>Situation:</u> Alex has BPD and has been feeling insecure about their partner, Jamie, after noticing Jamie has been quieter than usual. Alex fears Jamie might be losing interest or planning to leave. This fear triggers a need for reassurance.

Alex: "Hey, Jamie... can we talk for a minute?"

(Alex's voice sounds hesitant, and they seem anxious.)

Jamie: "Of course, what's on your mind?"

(Jamie looks up from their phone, noticing Alex's tone.)

Alex: "I don't know... I just feel like you've been kind of distant lately. Like, you're not texting me as much, and when we're together, it feels like you're not really present. Are you... mad at me or something?"

(Alex's words come out quickly, and their body language shows tension—fidgeting, avoiding eye contact.)

Jamie*: "I'm not mad at all, Alex. Work has just been really stressful this week, and I've been tired. I didn't mean to make you feel like I was ignoring you."*

(Jamie speaks calmly, trying to reassure Alex.)

Alex: *"But... are you sure? It feels like maybe you're pulling away. Like, do you still want to be with me? I just need to know if you're going to leave, because I can't handle being blindsided."*

(Alex's voice cracks slightly, and their fear of abandonment becomes more apparent.)

Jamie: *"Alex, I'm not going anywhere. I care about you, and I'm sorry if I made you feel like I didn't. I've just been caught up in my own stuff, but that doesn't change how I feel about you."*

(Jamie reaches out to hold Alex's hand, trying to provide physical reassurance.)

Alex: *"I just... I need to know you're not going to leave me. I can't stop thinking about it, and it's making me really anxious. Do you promise you're not going to leave?"*

(Alex's tone is pleading, and their eyes search Jamie's face for any sign of hesitation.)

Jamie: *"I promise, Alex. I'm not going to leave you. I know things feel overwhelming right now, but we're in this together. Let's talk more about how we can make sure you feel supported, okay?"*

(Jamie maintains eye contact and speaks gently, trying to convey sincerity and care.)

Alex: *"Okay... thank you. I'm sorry if I'm being too much. I just... I really needed to hear that."*

(Alex's shoulders relax slightly, and they let out a shaky breath, feeling a temporary sense of relief.)

Things to Observe – This highlights the **emotional vulnerability** and **relational challenges** that individuals with BPD often face.

Emotional Intensity: Alex's fear of abandonment is overwhelming and drives the need for constant reassurance. This isn't about being **"needy"** but about managing intense emotional pain.

Fear of Rejection: The fear of being left can feel **life-threatening to someone with BPD**, even if the threat isn't real. This fear often stems from past experiences of abandonment or neglect.

Reassurance as a Coping Mechanism: Seeking reassurance is a way for Alex to temporarily calm their anxiety and feel secure in the relationship. However, the relief is often short-lived, leading to repeated requests for reassurance.

Partner's Role: Jamie's calm and empathetic response helps de-escalate the situation. However, it's important to note that while reassurance can help in the moment, long-term support often involves helping the individual **develop self-soothing skills.**

2. A PATTERN OF UNSTABLE AND INTENSE INTERPERSONAL RELATIONSHIPS CHARACTERIZED BY ALTERNATING BETWEEN EXTREMES OF IDEALIZATION AND DEVALUATION.

People with BPD often struggle with relationships that swing between extremes. At one moment, they might idealize someone, seeing them as perfect and feeling intensely connected. However, a minor disagreement or perceived slight can quickly shift their perspective, leading them to devalue the same person, viewing them as uncaring or harmful. This pattern, often called **"splitting,"** creates a rollercoaster of emotions for both the individual and those around them. It reflects their difficulty in maintaining a balanced view of others, often rooted in early experiences of inconsistent or unreliable caregiving.

Situation: Taylor has BPD and has been in a close friendship with Jordan for several months. Initially, Taylor saw Jordan as the perfect friend, but after a minor disagreement, Taylor's perception shifts dramatically.

Phase 1: Idealization

(Taylor and Jordan are spending time together, and Taylor is expressing admiration for Jordan.)

Taylor: "Jordan, I just have to say... you're honestly the best friend I've ever had. Like, no one has ever understood me the way you do. You're so kind, and you always know how to make me feel better. I don't know what I'd do without you."

(Taylor's tone is enthusiastic, and they're smiling warmly at Jordan.)

Jordan: "Aw, Taylor, that means a lot. I'm really glad we're friends too. You're an amazing person, and I'm always here for you."

(Jordan smiles back, feeling appreciated but slightly overwhelmed by the intensity of Taylor's praise.)

Taylor: *"Seriously, you're like my rock. I feel like I can tell you anything, and you'll never judge me. You're just... perfect."*

(Taylor's words are filled with admiration, and they seem to place Jordan on a pedestal.)

Phase 2: Trigger Event

(A few days later, Jordan has to cancel plans with Taylor due to a work commitment. Taylor feels hurt and rejected.)

Taylor: *"Wait, you're canceling on me? But we've had these plans for days! I was really looking forward to this. Don't you care about spending time with me?"*

(Taylor's voice is tinged with hurt and frustration.)

Jordan: *"Taylor, I'm really sorry. It's just work—I can't get out of it. I'll make it up to you, I promise. It's not that I don't care."*

(Jordan sounds apologetic and tries to explain, but Taylor's emotions are escalating.)

Taylor: *"It feels like you're always too busy for me lately. Like, I'm not a priority to you at all. I thought you were different, but I guess I was wrong."*

(Taylor's tone shifts from hurt to anger, and their perception of Jordan begins to change.)

Phase 3: Devaluation

(Later that evening, Taylor texts Jordan, and the conversation takes a darker turn.)

Taylor: *"You know what, Jordan? I'm starting to think you're just like everyone else. You act like you care, but you don't. You're selfish, and you don't really care about me or my feelings."*

(Taylor's messages are filled with anger and disappointment, reflecting their shift from idealization to devaluation.)

Jordan: *"Taylor, that's not true. I do care about you. I'm really sorry I had to cancel, but it doesn't mean I don't value our friendship."*

(Jordan tries to reassure Taylor, but Taylor's emotions are too intense to be easily calmed.)

Taylor: "Whatever. I don't even know why I bother. You're just going to let me down like everyone else does. I thought you were different, but I guess I was wrong. I don't need this."

(Taylor's messages are harsh and final, reflecting their black-and-white thinking. They've gone from seeing Jordan as "perfect" to "selfish and uncaring.")

Phase 4: Aftermath

(The next day, Taylor feels guilty and tries to repair the relationship.)

Taylor: "Jordan, I'm so sorry about last night. I was really upset, and I didn't mean what I said. You're such an important person to me, and I don't want to lose you. Can we talk?"

(Taylor's tone is apologetic and vulnerable, reflecting their fear of losing the relationship.)

Jordan:" It's okay, Taylor. I know you were upset, and I'm not mad. Let's talk and figure things out. I care about you too, and I don't want this to come between us."

Things to Observe – This black-and-white thinking is a hallmark of BPD and can be confusing and hurtful for both parties.

<u>Trigger Event:</u> A minor conflict or **perceived rejection** (like canceling plans) can trigger a shift in perception. For Taylor, this feels like a betrayal, even though Jordan's actions were not intended to hurt them.

<u>Fear of Abandonment:</u> Underlying these shifts is a deep fear of abandonment. Taylor's intense reactions are driven by a need to protect themselves from perceived rejection or loss.

<u>Repair Attempts:</u> After the devaluation phase, individuals with BPD often feel guilt and try to repair the relationship. This cycle can repeat unless both parties work on communication and emotional regulation.

3. IDENTITY DISTURBANCE: MARKEDLY AND PERSISTENTLY UNSTABLE SELF-IMAGE OR SENSE OF SELF.

A stable sense of self is something many take for granted, but for individuals with BPD, their self-image can feel fragmented or constantly shifting. They may struggle to understand who they are, what they value, or what their goals are. This instability can lead to frequent changes in careers, friendships, hobbies, or even personal beliefs. It's as if they are searching for an anchor to define themselves but often feel lost or empty inside. This lack of a coherent identity can be deeply distressing and contribute to feelings of confusion and inadequacy.

Situation: Sam has BPD and is talking to their close friend, Casey, about their ongoing struggle with understanding who they are. Sam's self-image feels fragmented and constantly shifting, leading to confusion and distress.

Sam: "Casey, can I talk to you about something? I've been feeling really... lost lately. Like, I don't even know who I am anymore."

(Sam's voice is hesitant, and they seem visibly uncomfortable, fidgeting with their hands.)

Casey: "Of course, Sam. I'm here for you. What's going on?"

(Casey speaks gently, sensing Sam's distress.)

Sam: *"I just... I don't know how to explain it. It's like one day I feel like I'm this confident, outgoing person, and the next day I feel like I'm worthless and invisible. I don't even know which one is the real me. Does that make sense?"*

(Sam's tone is frustrated, and they struggle to articulate their feelings.)

Casey: *"It does make sense. It sounds like you're feeling really unsure about yourself right now. That must be really hard to deal with."*

(Casey validates Sam's feelings, offering empathy and support.)

Sam: *"It's more than unsure, though. It's like... I don't have a solid sense of who I am. I look at other people, and they seem so sure of themselves—like they know what they want, what they believe in, what they're good at. But me? I feel like I'm just... nothing. Or maybe I'm everything, and that's the problem. I don't know."*

(Sam's words are filled with confusion and despair, reflecting their unstable self-image.)

Casey: *"That sounds really overwhelming, Sam. It's okay to not have everything figured out. You're not alone in feeling this way, even if it seems like other people have it all together."*

(Casey tries to reassure Sam, emphasizing that it's okay to feel uncertain.)

Sam: *"But it's not just about figuring things out. It's like... I don't even know what I like or what I want. One day I'm obsessed with painting, and I think, 'This is it—this is who I am.' But then the next day, I can't even pick up a brush. I feel like a fraud. And it's not just hobbies—it's everything. My opinions, my values, even the way I act around people. It's like I'm constantly changing, and I don't know which version of me is real."*

(Sam's voice breaks slightly, and they look down, feeling ashamed of their confusion.)

Casey: *"Sam, it's okay to explore different parts of yourself. You don't have to fit into one box or be one specific person. It's okay to change and grow. But I can see how hard it is for you to feel so unsure. Have you thought about talking to someone who can help you work through this? Like a therapist?"*

(Casey offers support and gently suggests seeking professional help.)

Sam: *"I've thought about it, but I'm scared. What if they tell me there's something wrong with me? Or what if I can't figure it out, no matter how much I try? I just... I want* *to feel like a real person, you know? Like I'm not just a collection of random thoughts and feelings."*

(Sam's tone is vulnerable, and they express their fear of being judged or misunderstood.)

Casey: *"I get that, Sam. It's scary to feel like you don't know who you are. But you're not broken, and there's nothing wrong with you. You're just trying to figure things out, and that's okay. And you don't have to do it alone—I'm here for you, and there are people who can help you make sense of all this."*

(Casey reassures Sam, emphasizing that they're not alone and that help is available.)

Sam: *"Thanks, Casey. I don't know what I'd do without you. I just wish I could feel... solid, you know? Like I'm not constantly questioning everything about myself."*

(Sam's voice softens, and they express gratitude for Casey's support.)

Casey: *"I know, Sam. And I believe you'll get there. It might take time, but you're already taking steps by talking about it and being honest with yourself. That's really brave."*

(Casey offers encouragement, helping Sam feel a little more hopeful.)

Things to Observe –

<u>Fear of Judgment:</u> Sam is afraid of being judged or labeled as "broken," which can make it difficult for them to seek help. This fear often stems from past experiences of invalidation or criticism.

<u>Hope for Growth:</u> While identity disturbance is a challenging aspect of BPD, it's important to emphasize that with time, support, and therapy, individuals can develop a more stable and coherent sense of self.

4. IMPULSIVITY IN AT LEAST TWO AREAS THAT ARE POTENTIALLY SELF-DAMAGING (E.G., SPENDING, SEX, SUBSTANCE ABUSE, RECKLESS DRIVING, BINGE EATING).

Impulsivity in BPD often manifests in ways that can harm the individual, even if they don't intend it. This might include reckless spending sprees, engaging in unsafe sexual encounters, substance abuse, binge eating, or dangerous driving. These behaviors are typically attempts to cope with intense emotions or fill a void, but they often lead to negative consequences. It's crucial to recognize that these actions are not deliberate choices to self-sabotage but rather desperate efforts to manage overwhelming feelings or escape emotional pain.

Situation: Jamie has BPD and has been struggling with intense emotions lately. During a conversation with their friend Taylor, Jamie opens up about their recent impulsive behaviors.

Jamie: *"Taylor, I need to talk to you about something. I've been feeling so out of control lately, and I don't know what to do."*

(Jamie's voice is shaky, and they seem visibly distressed.)

Taylor: *"Of course, Jamie. I'm here for you. What's been going on?"*

(Taylor speaks gently, sensing Jamie's emotional state.)

Jamie: "I don't even know where to start. I've just been so overwhelmed, and I've been doing things I know I shouldn't. Like, last week, I went on this huge shopping spree. I maxed out my credit card buying stuff I don't even need—clothes, gadgets, random things. I didn't even think about it; I just did it. And now I'm drowning in debt, and I feel so stupid."

(Jamie's tone is filled with regret and frustration, and they avoid eye contact.)

Taylor: "That sounds really tough, Jamie. I know how hard it can be to resist those impulses when you're feeling overwhelmed. But you're not stupid—you're just trying to cope with something really difficult."

(Taylor validates Jamie's feelings while offering reassurance.)

Jamie: "It's not just the spending, though. I've also been drinking way too much. Like, every night this week, I've had way more than I should. I know it's bad for me, but when I'm drinking, it's like I can finally shut off my brain for a little while. The problem is, the next day I feel even worse, and then I just want to drink again to make it stop."

(Jamie's voice cracks, and they seem ashamed of their behavior.)

Taylor: *"Jamie, I'm really sorry you're feeling this way. It sounds like you're using spending and drinking to escape from something really painful. But I'm worried about you—these things can spiral out of control really quickly. Have you thought about talking to someone who can help you work through this?"*

(Taylor expresses concern and gently suggests seeking professional help.)

Jamie: *"I've thought about it, but I'm scared. What if they judge me? Or what if I can't stop, no matter what I do? I feel like I'm just stuck in this cycle, and I don't know how to get out."*

(Jamie's tone is vulnerable, and they express their fear of being judged or failing.)

Taylor: *"I get that, Jamie. It's scary to feel like you're out of control. But you're not alone in this, and there are people who can help you break the cycle. You don't have to figure it all out on your own."*

(Taylor reassures Jamie, emphasizing that they're not alone and that help is available.)

Jamie: *"I just don't know where to start. It feels like every time I try to do better, I end up falling back into the same patterns. I hate feeling like this."*

(Jamie's voice is filled with frustration and despair.)

Taylor: *"It's okay to feel that way, Jamie. Change is hard, and it doesn't happen overnight. But you're already taking a big step by talking about it. That's really brave. Maybe we can look into some resources together—like finding a therapist or a support group. You don't have to do this alone."*

(Taylor offers practical support and encouragement, helping Jamie feel a little more hopeful.)

Jamie: *"Thanks, Taylor. I don't know what I'd do without you. I just want to feel like I'm in control of my life again."*

(Jamie's voice softens, and they express gratitude for Taylor's support.)

Taylor: *"You'll get there, Jamie. It might take time, but I believe in you. And I'm here to help however I can."*

(Taylor offers reassurance and emphasizes their commitment to supporting Jamie.)

Things to Observe – This highlights the emotional turmoil and vulnerability that individuals with BPD often experience due to impulsivity.

<u>Impulsivity as a Coping Mechanism:</u> Jamie's impulsive behaviors—reckless spending and substance abuse—are attempts to cope with overwhelming emotions.

<u>Cycle of Shame and Guilt:</u> After the impulsive behavior, Jamie feels intense shame and guilt, which can fuel further impulsive actions as a way to escape those feelings.

<u>Hope for Change:</u> While impulsivity is a challenging aspect of BPD, it's important to emphasize that with time, support, and therapy, individuals can learn healthier coping mechanisms and regain a sense of control.

5. RECURRENT SUICIDAL BEHAVIOR, GESTURES, OR THREATS, OR SELF-MUTILATING BEHAVIOR.

One of the most distressing aspects of BPD is the tendency toward self-destructive behaviors, including suicidal gestures, threats, or self-harm (e.g., cutting or burning). These actions are often a way to express pain that feels too overwhelming to put into words or to regain a sense of control when emotions feel chaotic. While these behaviors can be alarming, they are not necessarily a desire to die but rather a cry for help or a way to cope with unbearable emotional suffering.

<u>**Situation:**</u> Alex has BPD and has been struggling with intense emotional pain. During a conversation with their close friend Riley, Alex opens up about their recurrent suicidal thoughts and self-harm behaviors.

Alex: "Riley, I need to talk to you about something... but I'm scared to say it out loud."

(Alex's voice is quiet and shaky, and they seem visibly anxious, fidgeting with their sleeves.)

Riley: "Alex, you know you can tell me anything. I'm here for you, no matter what."

(Riley speaks softly, offering reassurance and creating a safe space for Alex to open up.)

Alex: "I've been having these thoughts... about not wanting to be here anymore. It's like, everything feels so heavy, and I don't know how to keep carrying it. Sometimes I think about... ending things."

(Alex's voice breaks, and they look down, unable to meet Riley's eyes.)

Riley: "Alex, I'm so sorry you're feeling this way. That sounds really overwhelming. Thank you for trusting me enough to tell me. You're not alone in this, okay? I'm here with you."

(Riley responds with empathy, validating Alex's feelings and offering support.)

Alex: *"It's not just thoughts, though. Sometimes I... I hurt myself. Like, I'll cut my arms or legs. I know it's bad, but it's the only thing that makes the pain stop, even if it's just for a little while."*

(Alex's tone is filled with shame, and they pull their sleeves down further, as if trying to hide their scars.)

Riley: *"Alex, I can't imagine how much pain you must be in to feel like that's the only way to cope. But I'm really worried about you. You don't have to go through this alone. Have you thought about talking to someone who can help, like a therapist or counselor?"*

(Riley expresses concern and gently suggests seeking professional help.)

Alex: *"I've thought about it, but I'm scared. What if they don't understand? Or what if they try to lock me up or something? I don't want to lose control over my life."*

(Alex's voice is filled with fear, and they seem hesitant to consider professional help.)

Riley: *"I get that, Alex. It's scary to feel like you might lose control. But reaching out for help isn't about losing* control—it's about finding ways to feel better and stay safe. You deserve to feel better, and there are people who can help you get there."

(Riley reassures Alex, emphasizing that seeking help is a step toward healing, not a loss of autonomy.)

Alex: "I just don't know if I can stop. The thoughts keep coming back, and sometimes it feels like the only way out. I don't want to feel like this anymore, Riley."

(Alex's voice is filled with despair, and tears start to fall.)

Riley: "Alex, I can't promise that everything will be okay right away, but I can promise that I'll be here with you every step of the way. You're not alone in this. Let's figure out what you need to feel safe and supported. Maybe we can call a crisis line together or find a therapist who understands what you're going through."

(Riley offers practical support and emphasizes their commitment to being there for Alex.)

Alex: "I don't want to burden you with all of this. I feel like I'm too much to handle."

(Alex's tone is filled with guilt, and they seem to shrink into themselves.)

Riley: "You're not a burden, Alex. Not at all. You're my friend, and I care about you. I want to help you through *this because you matter to me. You're not too much—you're just going through a lot, and that's okay."*

(Riley reassures Alex, emphasizing their care and commitment to the friendship.)

Alex: *"Thank you, Riley. I don't know what I'd do without you. I just... I want to feel like life is worth living again."*

(Alex's voice softens, and they express gratitude for Riley's support.)

Riley: *"You will, Alex. It might take time, but I believe in you. And I'm here to help you get there. Let's take it one step at a time, okay?"*

(Riley offers encouragement and emphasizes hope for the future.)

Things to Observe – This highlights the emotional vulnerability and complexity of suicidal behavior and self-harm in BPD.

Emotional Pain Behind the Behavior: Alex's suicidal thoughts and self-harm are not attention-seeking but rather a response to overwhelming emotional pain. These behaviors are often a way to cope with feelings that feel unbearable.

<u>Shame and Fear:</u> Alex feels ashamed of their actions and fears being judged or misunderstood. This fear can make it difficult for them to seek help, even when they desperately need it.

<u>Hope for Healing:</u> While these behaviors are deeply distressing, it's important to emphasize that with the right support and treatment, individuals can learn healthier coping mechanisms and find hope for the future.

<u>Encouraging Professional Help:</u> Riley gently encourages Alex to seek professional help, emphasizing that it's a step toward healing and not a loss of control.

6. AFFECTIVE INSTABILITY DUE TO A MARKED REACTIVITY OF MOOD (E.G., INTENSE EPISODIC DYSPHORIA, IRRITABILITY, OR ANXIETY USUALLY LASTING A FEW HOURS AND ONLY RARELY MORE THAN A FEW DAYS).

Individuals with BPD often experience emotions that are intense, rapidly shifting, and difficult to manage. A minor event, such as a perceived rejection or criticism, can trigger overwhelming feelings of sadness, anger, or anxiety. These emotional episodes are usually short-lived, lasting a few hours or days, but they can feel all-consuming in the moment. This emotional volatility can make it challenging to maintain stability in daily life and relationships, as the individual may feel like they are on an emotional rollercoaster.

Situation: Jamie has BPD and has been experiencing intense mood swings throughout the day. During a conversation with their partner, Taylor, Jamie opens up about their emotional struggles.

Phase 1: Intense Episodic Dysphoria

(Jamie and Taylor are sitting together at home after a long day. Jamie seems visibly upset.)

Taylor: *"Hey, Jamie, you've been quiet all evening. Is everything okay?"*

(Taylor speaks gently, noticing Jamie's withdrawn demeanor.)

Jamie: *"I don't know... I just feel so sad all of a sudden. Like, this heavy weight is crushing me, and I can't shake it off. I was fine this morning, but now I feel like I'm drowning."*

(Jamie's voice is shaky, and they seem overwhelmed by their emotions.)

Taylor: "I'm so sorry you're feeling this way. Do you know what might have triggered it?"

(Taylor tries to understand the cause of Jamie's sudden mood shift.)

Jamie: "I don't know... I think it started when I got that email from work. They changed my schedule again, and it just made me feel like I don't matter. Like, no one cares about what I need or how I feel. And now I can't stop thinking about how worthless I am."

(Jamie's tone is filled with despair, and tears start to fall.)

Taylor: "Jamie, you're not worthless. I know it feels that way right now, but it's not true. You matter so much to me, and I'm here for you. Let's talk through this together, okay?"

(Taylor validates Jamie's feelings while offering reassurance and support.)

Phase 2: Irritability

(A few hours later, Jamie's mood shifts again. They become irritable and frustrated over a minor issue.)

Jamie: *"Why is this remote not working? Ugh, it's so annoying! Can't anything just work for once?"*

(Jamie's tone is sharp, and they seem agitated.)

Taylor: *"Here, let me try it. Maybe the batteries need to be replaced."*

(Taylor responds calmly, trying to help.)

Jamie: *"I don't need you to fix it! I'm not a child. I just... I can't deal with this right now. Everything is so frustrating!"*

(Jamie's voice is raised, and they seem disproportionately upset about the situation.)

Taylor: *"I'm sorry, Jamie. I didn't mean to upset you. I know you're having a tough day. Is there anything I can do to help?"*

(Taylor remains calm and empathetic, avoiding escalating the situation.)

Jamie: *"I don't know... I just feel so on edge. Like, everything is too much, and I can't handle it. I'm sorry for snapping at you. I don't mean to take it out on you."*

(Jamie's tone softens, and they express regret for their outburst.)

Taylor: "It's okay, Jamie. I know you're not trying to hurt me. You're just feeling overwhelmed, and that's okay. Let's take a deep breath together, okay?"

(Taylor offers reassurance and tries to help Jamie calm down.)

Phase 3: Anxiety

(Later that night, Jamie's mood shifts again, this time to intense anxiety.)

Jamie: "Taylor, I can't sleep. My mind is racing, and I feel like something terrible is going to happen. What if I mess up at work tomorrow? What if everyone hates me? I can't stop thinking about it."

(Jamie's voice is filled with panic, and they seem restless.)

Taylor: "Jamie, I'm here with you. You're safe, and everything is going to be okay. Let's focus on right now, okay? You don't have to figure everything out tonight."

(Taylor speaks soothingly, trying to ground Jamie in the present moment.)

Jamie: "I just feel like I'm falling apart. One minute I'm sad, the next I'm angry, and now I'm panicking. I don't know how to make it stop."

(Jamie's tone is desperate, and they seem exhausted by their emotional turmoil.)

Taylor: *"I know it feels like a lot right now, but these feelings will pass. You're not alone in this, Jamie. I'm here with you, and we'll get through it together."*

(Taylor offers comfort and emphasizes their support.)

Things to Observe – This highlights the emotional intensity and rapid mood shifts

Rapid Mood Shift : Jamie's mood shifts dramatically over the course of a few hours, from intense sadness to irritability to anxiety. This is a hallmark of affective instability in BPD.

Triggers and Reactivity: Minor events, like a work email or a malfunctioning remote, can trigger intense emotional reactions. These reactions often feel disproportionate to the situation but are very real to the individual experiencing them.

Emotional Exhaustion: The constant shifting of emotions can be exhausting for individuals with BPD.

Temporary Nature of Episodes: While these mood episodes are intense, they are usually short-lived, lasting a few hours or days. This can provide some hope that the emotional pain will pass.

7. CHRONIC FEELINGS OF EMPTINESS

Many people with BPD describe a persistent sense of emptiness, as if there is a void inside them that nothing can fill. This feeling can be profoundly isolating and may lead to efforts to distract themselves through impulsive behaviors or intense relationships. It's not just boredom or loneliness but a deeper, more existential ache that can make life feel meaningless or hollow. This emptiness often stems from a lack of a stable self-identity and unresolved emotional wounds from the past.

Situation: Alex has BPD and Sam, are sitting together at a coffee shop. Alex has been quiet and withdrawn all morning.

Sam: *"Hey, Alex, you've been really quiet today. Is everything okay?"*

Alex: *(shrugs, staring into their coffee) "I don't know. I just feel... empty. Like, there's this huge void inside me, and I can't figure out how to fill it. It's like I'm just going through the motions, but there's nothing there."*

Sam: *"What do you mean by 'nothing there'? Like, you're not feeling anything at all?"*

Alex: *"It's hard to explain. It's not that I'm sad or angry or anything specific. It's just... this constant numbness. Like, no matter what I do—whether I'm with friends, at work, or even doing something I usually enjoy—it feels like there's no point. I'm just... hollow."*

Sam: *"That sounds really hard. Does it ever go away?"*

Alex: (pauses, looking down) *"Not really. Sometimes it gets worse, especially when I'm alone. It's like I'm searching for something—anything—to make me feel alive, but nothing works. I've tried distractions, like binge-watching shows or scrolling through social media, but it just feels... meaningless. It's like I'm stuck in this endless void."*

Sam: *"Have you talked to your therapist about this?"*

Alex: *"Yeah, we've talked about it. She says it's part of the BPD, this chronic emptiness. But knowing that doesn't make it any easier to deal with. Sometimes I feel like I'm just... floating through life, like I don't even exist."*

Sam: *"That sounds really lonely. I'm sorry you're feeling this way. Is there anything I can do to help?"*

Alex: (smiles faintly) *"Just being here helps, honestly. It doesn't fix the emptiness, but it makes it a little easier to bear. Thanks for listening, Sam."*

Things to observe –

It Can Lead to a Sense of Meaninglessness: The emptiness often makes life feel pointless or meaningless, which can contribute to feelings of hopelessness or despair.

Be Patient: Chronic emptiness is a complex symptom that won't disappear overnight. Your consistent support can make a difference over time.

8. INAPPROPRIATE, INTENSE ANGER OR DIFFICULTY CONTROLLING ANGER (E.G., FREQUENT DISPLAYS OF TEMPER, CONSTANT ANGER, RECURRENT PHYSICAL FIGHTS).

Anger in BPD can be sudden, intense, and difficult to manage. Individuals may experience frequent outbursts, feel constantly irritable, or struggle with simmering resentment. This anger often arises from feelings of being misunderstood, invalidated, or abandoned. While it can be directed at others, it can also turn inward, contributing to feelings of guilt or shame. It's important to note that this anger is not a sign of a "bad temper" but rather a reflection of the individual's struggle to cope with intense emotions and unmet needs.

<u>Situation:</u> **A heated argument between Alex and Jordan, in a small, cluttered apartment. Alex has a**

history of anger issues, and Jordan is trying to help but is reaching their limit.

Jordan: *(calmly, but firmly) Alex, you can't keep doing this. You yelled at the barista for getting your order wrong, and then you almost got into a fight with that guy on the street. This isn't normal.*

Alex: *(clenching fists, voice rising) Oh, come on, Jordan! You weren't even there. That barista messed up my coffee twice, and that guy on the street? He bumped into me and didn't even apologize!*

Jordan: *(sighs, trying to stay composed) I get it, Alex. People can be frustrating. But you can't explode every time something doesn't go your way. It's like... it's like you're looking for a reason to be angry.*

Alex: *(pacing, voice getting louder) Looking for a reason? Are you serious? You think I "enjoy" this? You think I like feeling like I'm about to lose it all the time?*

Jordan: *(standing up, matching Alex's intensity) No, I don't think you enjoy it. But I do think you're not doing enough to control it. You keep saying you'll work on it, but nothing changes. It's exhausting, Alex. For you, for me, for everyone around you.*

Alex: *(stops pacing, glaring at Jordan) So what, you're saying I'm just some ticking time bomb? That I'm too much for you to handle?*

Jordan: *(softening, but still firm) I'm saying I care about you, but I can't keep watching you self-destruct. You need help, Alex. Real help. Not just promises to do better.*

Alex: *(voice cracking, a mix of anger and vulnerability) You think I don't know that? You think I don't hate myself every time I lose it? But it's like... it's like this fire just takes over, and I can't stop it.*

Jordan: *(stepping closer, gently) Then let someone help you put it out. Please. Before it burns everything down.*

Alex: *(looks away, fists unclenching slightly) I don't know if I can.*

Jordan: *(placing a hand on Alex's shoulder) You don't have to do it alone. But you have to try.*

Things to observe – Try to observe

9. TRANSIENT, STRESS-RELATED PARANOID IDEATION OR SEVERE DISSOCIATIVE SYMPTOMS.

Under extreme stress, individuals with BPD may experience **temporary paranoid thoughts** or

dissociation. Paranoia might involve feeling suspicious of other's intentions or believing they are being mistreated without evidence. Dissociation, can feel like being disconnected from oneself or the world, as if watching life from a distance. These symptoms are often triggered by overwhelming stress or trauma reminders and serve as a way to escape emotional pain. While these experiences can be frightening, they are typically short-lived and resolve once the stress subsides.

<u>Situation:</u> Late at night in a dimly lit living room. Emma, has been under intense stress at work and in her personal life. Her partner, Sam, notices her increasingly erratic behavior and tries to talk to her.

Sam: *(softly, sitting across from Emma) Emma, you've been... distant lately. Like you're not really here. And last night, when you thought someone was watching us through the window... there was no one there.*

Emma :*(hugging herself, avoiding eye contact) I know what I saw, Sam. You don't understand. They're always watching. They know what I've done.*

Sam: *(leaning forward, concerned) What you've done? Emma, you haven't done anything wrong. What are you talking about?*

Emma: *(voice trembling, eyes darting around the room) You don't get it. They're listening. They're always listening. Even now. (whispers) They can hear us.*

Sam: *(gently) Emma, no one's listening. It's just us. You're safe here.*

Emma: *(suddenly standing, agitated) Safe? How can I be safe when they're everywhere? At work, on the street, even in our house. They're waiting for me to slip up.*

Sam: *(standing slowly, trying to stay calm) Who's waiting, Emma? Who are you talking about?*

Emma: (pacing, voice rising) I don't know! But they're there. I can feel it. It's like... like I'm not even me anymore. Like I'm watching myself from the outside, and I can't stop it.

Sam: (reaching out, but not touching her) Emma, that sounds like... like you're under so much stress that your mind is playing tricks on you. You're not yourself right now.

Emma *:(stopping, staring at Sam with wide eyes) What if I'm never myself again? What if this is who I am now?*

Sam*: (firmly, but with compassion) That's not true. This isn't you. This is the stress, the exhaustion, whatever you're carrying. But you don't have to carry it alone. Let me help you.*

Emma: *(breaking down, sinking to the floor) I don't know what Sam is real anymore,. I don't know if I can trust my own mind.*

Sam: *(kneeling beside her, voice steady) Then trust me. Just for now. Let's get through this together.*

Brainstorm, Try to observe.

CHAPTER THREE
FRAGILE FOUNDATION

Childhood is often referred to as the foundation upon which our future selves are built. For individuals with Borderline Personality Disorder (BPD), this foundation can be fragile, fractured by **early experiences of trauma and neglect**. Many people living with BPD report histories of physical or sexual abuse during their formative years, inflicted by trusted caregivers or family members. This betrayal of trust creates deep-seated insecurities and emotional scars that can last a lifetime.

The trauma endured in childhood lays the groundwork for many of the core issues seen in BPD. The fragile foundation leads to profound **emotional instability, intense fears of abandonment, and difficulties in forming healthy relationships**. These individuals often struggle with a **pervasive sense of emptiness** and may engage in impulsive behaviors as they attempt to cope with the lingering pain and fill the void left by early neglect or abuse.

Childhood trauma isn't limited to overt acts of violence or abuse. Many with BPD have experienced other forms of adversity, such as domestic violence, parental separation, or emotional neglect. These experiences can be just as damaging, leaving children feeling unloved, unprotected, and invisible. The lack of proper attention and care from parents or caregivers creates a **void—a space of unmet needs and unfulfilled emotional support.** As these children grow into adults, they carry the unresolved pain and unmet needs with them. The fear of abandonment becomes a central theme, leading to intense, unstable relationships and a desperate need for validation and reassurance. The impulsivity often seen in BPD can be a reaction to these fears, a way to numb the pain or distract from the overwhelming feelings of emptiness.

Recognizing the impact of childhood trauma is a crucial step toward healing and finding ways to manage the disorder. It's not about blaming the past but about understanding it and finding compassion for the child within who endured so much. Through therapy, self-reflection, and support, individuals with BPD can begin to rebuild their foundation, creating a more stable and fulfilling life.

DEVELOPMENT OF SELF- HARMING BEHAVIOR

In Borderline Personality Disorder (BPD), self-harming and suicidal behaviors are often deeply linked to childhood experiences, particularly those involving trauma, neglect, or inconsistent caregiving.

1. Emotional Dysregulation from Early Childhood

Children who grow up in invalidating environments (where their emotions are dismissed, punished, or ignored) may struggle to regulate emotions later in life. When distress becomes overwhelming, the brain searches for immediate ways to reduce the pain. Self-harm and suicidal behaviors often function as maladaptive coping mechanisms to deal with this emotional overload.

Emotions in BPD escalate rapidly due to a **hypersensitive amygdala** (the brain's emotional processing center). **The prefrontal cortex** (responsible for impulse control and rational decision-making) struggles to regulate these emotions. This creates emotional storms where the person feels unbearable pain and seeks an immediate escape, leading to self-harm or suicidal thoughts.

2. Attachment Trauma and Fear of Abandonment

Many people with BPD experience unstable relationships due to deep fears of abandonment, which often stem from early attachment trauma. If a child's caregivers were unpredictable, emotionally unavailable, or abusive, they may develop a heightened sensitivity to rejection, leading to self-destructive behaviors in adulthood.

3. <u>Dissociation and Feeling "Unreal"</u>

Childhood trauma can lead to dissociation (a sense of detachment from reality or oneself).Self-harm can be a way to "feel real" again by experiencing physical sensations.

4. <u>Learned Coping Mechanisms</u>

If a child witnesses self-harm or suicide attempts in their family or is not taught healthy ways to cope with distress, they may learn to use self-harm as a way to regulate emotions.

5. <u>Shame and Self-Hatred</u>

Childhood emotional abuse or constant criticism can create deep feelings of worthlessness. Self-harm may become a way to punish oneself or express self-hatred.

6. <u>Impulsivity and Lack of Emotional Safety</u>

A history of childhood neglect or unstable caregiving can impair impulse control. In moments of intense distress, the inability to self-soothe leads to impulsive acts like self-harm or suicide attempts.

THE PURPOSE OF SELF-HARM IN BPD

Self-harm (e.g., cutting, burning, scratching, hitting) is not always about wanting to die. It serves different psychological purposes:

A. <u>Emotional Regulation (Reducing Overwhelming Emotions)</u>

When emotions feel out of control, physical pain provides a sense of relief or grounding. The act distracts from emotional pain by shifting focus to the body. It can act as a "reset button" for emotional distress.

B. <u>Ending Emotional Numbness (Feeling Real Again)</u>

Many people with BPD experience dissociation (feeling disconnected from reality or their body). Self-harm can be a way to "wake up" from this numbness and feel alive again.

C. <u>Self-Punishment (Reinforcing Negative Beliefs)</u>

If someone grew up with childhood emotional abuse, neglect, or invalidation, they may internalize beliefs like "I am bad" or "I deserve pain." Self-harm may act as a way to punish oneself for perceived mistakes or self-hatred.

D. <u>Seeking Help or Validation (But Feeling Ashamed of It)</u>

Some people self-harm as a cry for help when they struggle to express emotional pain verbally. However, afterward, they often feel guilt and shame for doing it, leading to further distress.

THE NEUROLOGY BEHIND SELF-HARM: HOW IT BECOMES ADDICTIVE

Self-harm works like an addictive behavior because of how the brain processes pain and reward.

A. <u>Endorphin Release (Pain as a Temporary Relief)</u>

When the skin is cut or burned, the body releases endorphins (natural painkillers) to numb the pain. These chemicals create a temporary sense of calm or euphoria, reinforcing the urge to do it again.

B. <u>Dopamine and Habit Formation</u>

Self-harm activates dopamine, the brain's reward chemical, making it feel momentarily "good." Over time, the brain associates self-harm with emotional relief, making it a compulsive behavior.

C. <u>Stress and Cortisol Overload</u>

People with BPD often have chronic high levels of cortisol (stress hormone). Self-harm can temporarily reduce cortisol, giving the illusion of relief—but it worsens stress cycles over time.

SUICIDAL BEHAVIOR IN BPD: WHY IT HAPPENS

A. <u>Suicidal Ideation as a Coping Mechanism</u>

Many people with BPD don't necessarily want to die—they want an end to emotional suffering. Suicidal thoughts often emerge during intense emotional breakdowns, feeling like there is no escape.

B. <u>Impulsivity and Emotional Storms</u>

Because impulse control is weak, suicide attempts in BPD can be sudden and unplanned. A person may genuinely not want to die but act impulsively in a moment of extreme distress.

C. <u>Fear of Abandonment Triggering Suicide Threats or Attempts</u>

If someone with BPD feels abandoned or rejected, it can cause suicidal urges. This is **not always manipulation**—it's often an intense emotional response to feeling unlovable or unworthy.

THE MISUNDERSTOOD REALITY OF MOOD SHIFTS

One of the most common misconceptions about people with Borderline Personality Disorder (BPD) is the belief that we are being dramatic or pretentious when our moods shift suddenly and intensely. To an outsider, it might seem like we are overreacting or seeking attention. However, the reality is far more complex and deeply rooted in the emotional turbulence that defines BPD.

For those of us living with BPD, emotions can change with a velocity and intensity that is hard to comprehend unless experienced firsthand. A moment of calm can quickly spiral into anxiety, sadness, or anger, often triggered by seemingly small events. This isn't about creating drama; it's about the way our brains are wired to process emotions. These sudden shifts are not under our control and can be as surprising to us as they are to those around us.

Imagine living in a world where every emotion feels amplified—where a simple disagreement feels like rejection, where a kind word can bring immense joy, and where a minor setback can feel like the end of the world. This is the emotional landscape of BPD. Our reactions are not exaggerated or fabricated; they are genuine, albeit intense, responses to the world around us.

It's essential to understand that these mood changes are not intentional. We are not trying to manipulate or deceive; we are navigating a rollercoaster of emotions that can be exhausting and overwhelming. What we need is empathy, patience, and support from those around us, not judgment or dismissal.

By recognizing that these mood shifts are a part of who we are, rather than a choice or a performance, you can begin to see the person behind the emotions. Understanding this can help foster deeper connections and provide a more supportive environment for both parties in the relationship.

So, next time you see someone with BPD experiencing a sudden emotional shift, remember: **they are not being dramatic or pretentious.** They are simply living with the challenges of a disorder that affects their emotional regulation. Your understanding and compassion can make a world of difference.

TRAUMA AND ATTACHMENT RELATIONSHIPS

Complex trauma has a profound impact on how individuals form attachments and process emotions. In a healthy development process, when a person feels threatened or distressed, their natural response is to seek comfort from caregivers. This instinct is driven by the brain's reward system, which helps regulate stress and reinforces feelings of safety and support.

However, trauma can disrupt this pattern, especially when caregivers are inconsistent, unresponsive, or even harmful. Instead of confidently seeking support, individuals may develop two extreme coping mechanisms: hyperactivation or deactivation of their attachment system. Hyperactivating strategies involve an intense need for closeness and reassurance, often leading to anxiety in relationships. Deactivating strategies involve emotional withdrawal and a reluctance to rely on others, stemming from the belief that caregivers are unreliable or even dangerous.

Many trauma survivors experience both of these responses, creating a **cycle of approach-avoidance** in relationships—wanting connection but fearing it at the same time. This instability can make it difficult for them to seek help, including from mental health professionals.

Research suggests that individuals with borderline personality disorder (BPD) often show patterns of **preoccupied attachment** (associated with hyperactivation) or **disorganized attachment** (a mix of hyperactivation and deactivation). These attachment difficulties contribute to the emotional instability and relationship struggles commonly seen in BPD.

(Smits ML, Luyten P, Feenstra DJ, Bales DL, Kamphuis JH, Dekker JJ, Verheul R, Busschbach JJ. Trauma and outcomes of mentalization-based therapy for individuals with borderline personality disorder. American journal of psychotherapy. 2022 Jan 1;75(1):12-20.)

Growing up in an abusive or neglectful environment can make it difficult for a person to develop the ability to understand and regulate their emotions, a skill known as mentalizing. This is especially true in cases of attachment trauma, where a child lacks a responsive caregiver to help them manage stress and emotional distress. Without this support, individuals may struggle to process their experiences in a healthy way.

For those with borderline personality disorder (BPD) and a history of trauma, this often leads to intense feelings of loneliness and isolation. They may also develop a distorted view of themselves and others, seeing people in extreme terms—either as **"bad," "evil," "neglected," or "unworthy."** These perceptions can drive behaviors that unintentionally reinforce past trauma, leading to patterns of reenactment and revictimization.

Revictimization refers to the phenomenon where an individual who has experienced trauma, particularly abuse or neglect, is more likely to experience further victimization in the future. Revictimization happens when a person, often unconsciously, finds themselves in harmful situations similar to past experiences. This is thought to result from a deeply ingrained pattern where the abuser is seen as both a source of fear and pain, yet also as someone who provides care and love. This contradiction creates **a cycle of internal conflict—wanting closeness but also fearing it**—which is a key feature of disorganized attachment. This pattern is especially common in individuals with BPD, making it difficult for them to form stable, healthy relationships.

HYPERACTIVATING STRATEGIES

Hyperactivating strategies are characterized by intense efforts to seek proximity, support, and reassurance from others. These strategies are often employed when an individual feels threatened, abandoned, or insecure. It is characterized by -

1. **<u>Emotional Intensity:</u>** Individuals may experience and express emotions in an exaggerated manner. This can include intense fear of abandonment, anger, or sadness.

2. **<u>Closeness Seeking:</u>** There is a strong desire for closeness and reassurance from others. This can manifest as clinginess, frequent contact, or demands for attention.

3. **<u>Fear of Abandonment:</u>** A pervasive fear of being abandoned or rejected can drive behaviors aimed at preventing real or perceived abandonment.

4. **<u>Impulsivity:</u>** In an attempt to alleviate emotional distress, individuals may engage in impulsive behaviors such as self-harm, substance abuse, or reckless actions.

5. **<u>Idealization and Devaluation:</u>** Relationships may be characterized by alternating between idealizing others (seeing them as perfect and all-loving) and devaluing them (seeing them as neglectful or harmful).

Hyperactivating strategies serve to maintain proximity to attachment figures, ensuring that the individual feels safe and supported. These strategies are often a response to inconsistent caregiving in childhood, where the individual learned that intense expressions of need were necessary to elicit care.

DEACTIVATING STRATEGIES

Deactivating strategies involve efforts to minimize attachment needs and suppress emotions. These strategies are used to create emotional distance and avoid perceived threats or vulnerabilities.

1. **Emotional Suppression:** Individuals may suppress or deny their emotions, particularly those related to vulnerability or neediness.

2. **Avoidance of Closeness:** There is a tendency to avoid close relationships or to maintain emotional distance in relationships. This can manifest as aloofness, detachment, or avoidance of intimacy.

3. **Self-Reliance:** A strong emphasis on self-reliance and independence, often to the point of rejecting help or support from others.

4. **Dismissiveness:** Individuals may dismiss the importance of relationships or downplay their need for others.

5. **Isolation:** There may be a preference for solitude and a tendency to withdraw from social interactions, especially in times of stress.

Deactivating strategies serve to protect the individual from the pain of rejection or abandonment by minimizing attachment needs and avoiding emotional vulnerability. These strategies often develop in response to experiences where attachment figures were consistently unavailable or rejecting, leading the individual to learn that relying on others is unsafe.

In BPD, individuals may oscillate between hyperactivating and deactivating strategies, leading to unstable and tumultuous relationships. This oscillation reflects the underlying fear of abandonment and the difficulty in regulating emotions.

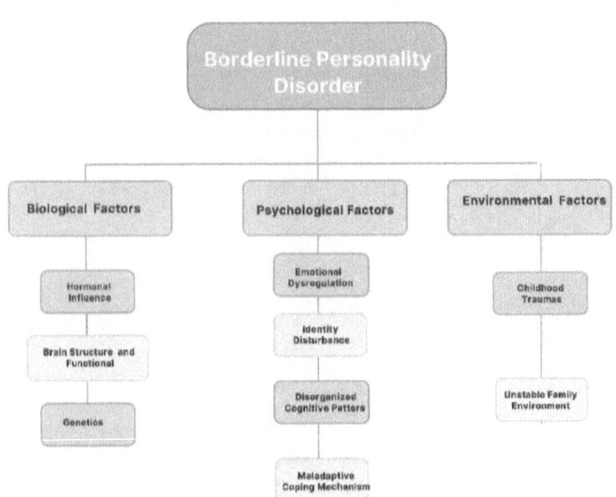

BIOLOGICAL FACTORS

Biological factors refer to the physical and genetic aspects that may predispose someone to developing BPD. These factors are not deterministic but can increase vulnerability when combined with other influences.

GENETICS

Family Studies-Research shows that BPD tends to run in families. Individuals with a first-degree relative (parent, sibling, or child) who has BPD are more likely to develop the disorder themselves.

Heritability - Twin studies suggest that genetic factors account for approximately 40-60% of the risk for BPD. However, no single gene has been identified as the cause; rather, it's likely a combination of multiple genes interacting with environmental factors.

BRAIN STRUCTURE AND FUNCTION

Amygdala- The amygdala, which regulates emotions, is often hyperactive in individuals with BPD. This may explain the intense emotional reactions and difficulty regulating emotions.

Prefrontal Cortex - The prefrontal cortex, responsible for decision-making, impulse control, and emotional regulation, may be less active or structurally different in people with BPD. This can contribute to impulsivity and difficulty managing emotions.

Hippocampus - The hippocampus, involved in memory and emotional processing, may be smaller in individuals with BPD. This could affect how they process and recall emotional experiences.

Neurotransmitters- Imbalances in neurotransmitters like serotonin, dopamine, and norepinephrine may play a role in mood instability, impulsivity, and emotional dysregulation.

HORMONAL INFLUENCES

Stress Response - Individuals with BPD often have an overactive hypothalamic-pituitary-adrenal (HPA) axis, which regulates the body's response to stress. This can lead to heightened sensitivity to stress and difficulty calming down after emotional triggers.

ENVIRONMENTAL FACTORS

Environmental factors refer to external influences, particularly during childhood, that can contribute to the development of BPD. These factors often interact with biological vulnerabilities.

CHILDHOOD TRAUMA

Abuse - Physical, sexual, or emotional abuse during childhood is strongly associated with BPD. Trauma can disrupt emotional development and lead to difficulties in forming healthy relationships.

Neglect - Emotional neglect or abandonment by caregivers can create a sense of insecurity and fear of rejection, which are core features of BPD.

Invalidation- Growing up in an environment where emotions are dismissed, criticized, or punished can lead to emotional dysregulation and a lack of trust in one's own feelings.

UNSTABLE FAMILY ENVIRONMENT

Parental Conflict - High levels of conflict, divorce, or inconsistent parenting can create an unstable environment, making it difficult for a child to develop a stable sense of self.

Attachment Issues- Insecure attachment styles, such as anxious or disorganized attachment, are common in individuals with BPD. These attachment patterns often stem from early relationships with caregivers.

SOCIOCULTURAL FACTORS

Social Isolation - A lack of social support or feelings of isolation during formative years can exacerbate emotional difficulties.

Cultural Expectations - Societal pressures or cultural norms that stigmatize emotional expression may contribute to the development of BPD symptoms.

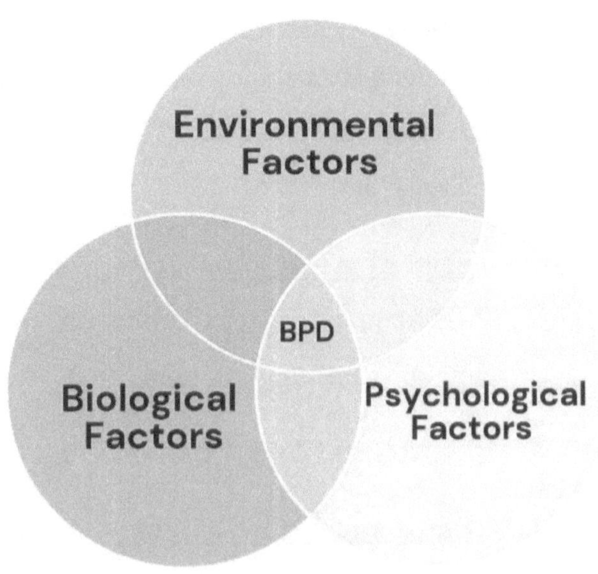

PSYCHOLOGICAL FACTORS

Psychological factors involve the internal processes and personality traits that contribute to the development and maintenance of BPD.

EMOTIONAL DYSREGULATION

Intense Emotions - Individuals with BPD often experience emotions more intensely and for longer durations than others. This heightened emotional sensitivity can make it difficult to regulate feelings.

Difficulty Self-Soothing - A lack of effective coping mechanisms for managing distress can lead to impulsive behaviors or self-harm as a way to cope.

IDENTITY DISTURBANCE

<u>**Unstable Self-Image**</u>- Many individuals with BPD struggle with a fragmented or unstable sense of self. This can lead to frequent changes in goals, values, and relationships.

<u>**Fear of Abandonment**</u>- A deep-seated fear of being abandoned or rejected often drives behaviors such as clinginess, manipulation, or rapid relationship cycling.

DISORGANIZED COGNITIVE PATTERNS

<u>**Black-and-White Thinking**</u> - Splitting, or seeing things in extremes (e.g., all good or all bad), is a common cognitive pattern in BPD. This can lead to unstable relationships and difficulty seeing nuance in situations.

<u>**Negative Self-Perception**</u> - Many individuals with BPD struggle with chronic feelings of worthlessness or self-hatred, which can perpetuate emotional distress.

MALADAPTIVE COPING MECHANISMS

<u>**Impulsivity**</u>- Impulsive behaviors, such as substance abuse, reckless spending, or self-harm, are often used as a way to cope with overwhelming emotions.

<u>**Self-Sabotage**</u> - Fear of failure or rejection can lead to behaviors that undermine personal goals or relationships.

MYTHS AND MISCONCEPTIONS ABOUT BORDERLINE PERSONALITY DISORDER

Misinformation and stigma often surround BPD, leading to harmful stereotypes and barriers to effective treatment.

- **Myth:** People with BPD Are Manipulative

***The Misconception** - Individuals with the disorder are manipulative, using their emotions or behaviors to control others.*

The Truth- *Behaviors that may appear manipulative, such as self-harm or intense emotional reactions, are often expressions of deep emotional pain or fear of abandonment. These actions are not calculated attempts to control others but rather desperate attempts to cope with overwhelming emotions.*

People with BPD are not inherently manipulative. They are often struggling with intense emotions and a lack of effective coping mechanisms. Compassion and understanding can go a long way in supporting them.

- **Myth:** BPD Is Untreatable

***The Misconception-** BPD is a lifelong, untreatable condition with no hope for recovery.*

The Truth- BPD is highly treatable. With the right therapy, many individuals experience significant improvement in their symptoms and quality of life. Research shows that a majority of people with BPD achieve remission over time.

Recovery is possible. While the journey may be challenging, many individuals with BPD go on to lead fulfilling, meaningful lives.

- **Myth:** BPD Only Affects Women

The Misconception - BPD is often portrayed as a "women's disorder," leading to the misconception that it primarily or exclusively affects women.

The Truth- While BPD is diagnosed more frequently in women, men can and do experience BPD as well. Men with BPD may be underdiagnosed or misdiagnosed with other conditions, such as antisocial personality disorder or substance use disorders.

- **Myth:** People with BPD Are Dangerous

The Misconception- Media portrayals often depict individuals with BPD as violent or dangerous, contributing to fear and stigma.

The Truth - While individuals with BPD may struggle with impulsivity or emotional dysregulation, they are not inherently dangerous. In fact, they are more likely to harm themselves than others. Self-harm and suicidal behaviors are more common in BPD than violence toward others.

- **Myth:** BPD Is Just "Bad Behavior"

The Misconception - Some people believe that BPD is simply a result of poor choices or a lack of self-control, dismissing it as "bad behavior."

The Truth - BPD is a complex mental health condition rooted in biological, psychological, and environmental factors. It is not a choice or a character flaw but a legitimate disorder that requires understanding and treatment. Reducing BPD to "bad behavior" ignores the profound emotional pain and struggles that individuals with the disorder face. Empathy and education are key to breaking down this harmful myth.

Myth: People with BPD Can't Have Healthy Relationships

The Misconception- It is often assumed that individuals with BPD are incapable of maintaining healthy, stable relationships.

The Truth - While relationships can be challenging for individuals with BPD, they are not doomed to fail. With therapy and support, many people with BPD learn to build and maintain healthy, fulfilling relationships.

Relationships with someone who has BPD may require patience, communication, and boundaries, but they can be deeply rewarding. Love and connection are possible for everyone, including those with BPD.

Myth: People with BPD Are Attention-Seeking

The Misconception - Behaviors such as self-harm or emotional outbursts are often dismissed as "attention-seeking."

The Truth - These behaviors are typically cries for help, not attempts to gain attention. Individuals with BPD are often in profound emotional pain and may not know how to express their needs in healthier ways. Dismissing someone's struggles as attention-seeking can further isolate them

Myth: BPD Is a Life Sentence

The Truth- Many individuals with BPD experience significant improvement over time, especially with appropriate treatment. Remission is possible, and many people go on to live fulfilling lives.

Myth: Only "Weak" People Develop BPD.

__The Misconception__ - There is a harmful belief that BPD is a sign of weakness or a lack of resilience.

The Truth- BPD is not a reflection of weakness. It is a complex condition influenced by genetics, trauma, and environmental factors. Many individuals with BPD are incredibly resilient, having survived significant adversity. Strength and resilience are not the absence of struggle but the ability to keep going despite it. People with BPD are often some of the strongest individuals you will meet.

BREAKING THE STIGMA

The myths and misconceptions surrounding BPD contribute to stigma, shame, and barriers to treatment. By challenging these myths and replacing them with accurate information, we can create a more compassionate and understanding world for individuals with BPD. Education is the first step toward breaking the stigma and ensuring that everyone affected by BPD receives the support and care they deserve.

"BPD is not a character flaw, a choice, or a life sentence. It is a treatable condition, and recovery is possible. Replace judgment with empathy and misinformation with understanding."

CHAPTER FOUR
THE PUSH AND PULLS: RELATIONSHIP DYNAMICS

A relationship with someone who has Borderline Personality Disorder (BPD) is a paradox—intensely beautiful yet deeply challenging. It can feel like an emotional rollercoaster, filled with passion, love, chaos, and pain. Individuals with borderline personality disorder (BPD) often experience significant instability in their emotions, thoughts, motivations, and behaviors. This instability can lead to turbulent interpersonal relationships and ongoing difficulties in forming and maintaining healthy bonds. Key factors contributing to these challenges include **attachment insecurity**, **difficulties in maintaining a stable sense of identity**, **impaired mentalization** (the ability to understand one's own and others' mental states), and **heightened emotional reactivity**. Together, these elements disrupt relationship dynamics through patterns such as choosing unsuitable partners, conflicting relationship goals, poor communication, struggles with regulating risk and trust, and even instances of physical and psychological conflict.

For individuals with Borderline Personality Disorder (BPD), relationships often hold a profound significance, becoming central to their emotional well-being. While these connections can be deeply healing but they can also amplify past traumas or leads to new traumas. People with BPD (PwBPD) tend to develop behavioral patterns where they invest everything into the person they long to be loved and accepted by. Their desire for closeness can lead to intense expressions of affection, sometimes described as "love bombing," followed by sudden feelings of anger, disappointment, or withdrawal if they perceive they are not being understood. This perception is often shaped by the other person's responses, which they may interpret in a heightened or distorted way or **Hypermentalizing**. These moments can trigger overwhelming fears of abandonment, further fueling insecurity. Over time, this can contribute to the development of an insecure attachment style, leaving them feeling emotionally unfulfilled and at a disadvantage in seeking the connection and reassurance they deeply crave.

Research shows that individuals with BPD tend to experience episodic relationship instability, characterized by cycles of breaking up and reconciling. In fact, nearly 70% of couples with a BPD partner reported incidents of relationship termination followed by reunification at least once within a six-month period.

Compared to couples without a BPD partner, these relationships exhibit distinct differences across several psychosocial factors, including attachment styles, patterns of intimate violence, communication difficulties, psychological distress, and lower relationship satisfaction. Insecure attachment styles are particularly prominent, marked by significant difficulties in managing emotions. This can result in a chaotic **pattern of hyperactivation** (intensified emotional reactions, clinging behavior) and **deactivation** (emotional withdrawal, avoidance).

Individuals with BPD often live with a deep, pervasive fear of abandonment and dependency, leading to alternating behaviors such as outbursts of rage, devaluation of their partners, and avoidance. These cycles lock couples into harmful, repetitive patterns that damage relationship quality and long-term stability. Understanding these dynamics with clarity and compassion is essential for addressing the challenges couples face and identifying ways to foster healthier, more stable connections.

Bouchard S, Sabourin S, Lussier Y, Villeneuve E. Relationship quality and stability in couples when one partner suffers from borderline personality disorder. Journal of marital and family therapy. 2009 Oct;35(4):446-55.

Studies showed nearly early half of the men romantically involved with women suffering from BPD were found to develop a personality disorder overtime. It is equally challenging for Non- BPD partner to make the relationship workout and in most cases, they feel better to get out of these kind of relationship as they can't see a long term stability with the BPD partner. But there have be instances where relationships lasted long , in those cases , it was found that a lot of Sacrifices , Maturity and commitment was from both the sides.

Being in a relationship with someone who has Borderline Personality Disorder (BPD) can be both deeply intense and emotionally exhausting for the non-BPD partner. The effects depend on the partner's personality, emotional resilience, and ability to set boundaries. Here's how it often impacts them:

1. Emotional Burnout

The intensity of emotions in the relationship can be overwhelming. The non-BPD partner may feel like they're always walking on eggshells, afraid of triggering an emotional outburst. Constant reassurance-giving and managing crises can be draining.

2. Psychological Confusion (Gaslighting & Cognitive Dissonance)

Due to splitting (black-and-white thinking), the BPD partner may switch from idealization to devaluation quickly. One day, they feel loved and cherished. The next, they are blamed, ignored, or even treated as the enemy. This inconsistency can lead to self-doubt, confusion, and questioning reality.

3. Guilt & Responsibility for Partner's Emotions

The BPD partner may externalize their emotions, making their partner feel responsible for their pain. The non-BPD partner might feel guilty for not being able to "fix" things. They may stay in an unhealthy dynamic because they fear abandoning their BPD partner, especially if there are threats of self-harm.

4. Loss of Self-Identity & Codependency

Many non-BPD partners lose themselves trying to manage their partner's emotions. They may prioritize their BPD partner's needs over their own, leading to codependency. Over time, they might feel like they don't have their own emotions, goals, or independence anymore.

5. Anxiety & Hypervigilance

The unpredictability of emotional reactions in a BPD relationship can cause the partner to develop anxiety and hyperawareness.

They may:

- Constantly check their phone, fearing an emotional text.
- Avoid certain topics or situations to prevent an argument.
- Feel on edge, always anticipating the next emotional storm.

6. Feeling Unappreciated or Emotionally Drained

Despite giving unconditional support, the non-BPD partner may feel like it's never enough. Love and affection may feel conditional, depending on the BPD partner's current emotions. Over time, they may feel emotionally drained, resentful, or even numb.

7. Isolation from Friends & Family

The intensity of the relationship may cause the non-BPD partner to withdraw from others. Some BPD partners (especially those with abandonment fears) may unconsciously discourage or sabotage external relationships. The non-BPD partner might feel alone with no one to talk to about their struggles.

8. Developing Mental Health Struggles

Many non-BPD partners develop depression, anxiety, PTSD, or self-doubt after prolonged exposure to emotional turbulence. Some even start mirroring BPD behaviors, experiencing emotional dysregulation themselves.

SIMPLE THINGS WHICH MATTERS THE MOST

- Small triggers (like a delayed text) can lead to emotional outbursts, feelings of abandonment, or sudden coldness. Arguments can escalate quickly, even over minor misunderstandings.

- Even in a stable relationship, a person with BPD may constantly fear being abandoned. This can lead to intense jealousy, neediness, or self-sabotaging behaviors (e.g., pushing you away to "test" your love). They might interpret normal distance as rejection, leading to emotional distress.
- Many people with BPD struggle with self-harm, reckless actions, or substance abuse. Some may threaten self-harm during arguments, making their partner feel responsible for their safety. Impulsive decisions (like sudden breakups, financial recklessness, or emotional outbursts) can add instability to the relationship.
- Due to past trauma or emotional wounds, BPD partners may struggle to fully trust even the most loyal partners. They might suspect betrayal, misinterpret actions, or accuse their partner of things they haven't done. Constantly reassuring them can become exhausting over time.

THE BEAUTY OF HAVING A BPD PARTNER

1. Deep & Intense Love

A BPD partner loves with all their heart. When they care, they do so with unmatched intensity. They make their partner feel like the most special, cherished person in the world. When they feel safe, they are incredibly loyal, affectionate, and devoted.

2. Emotional Depth & Vulnerability

People with BPD experience emotions more deeply than most. When they open up, they show raw, unfiltered emotions that can create a profound bond. They appreciate and value emotional intimacy like no one else.

3. Excitement & Passion

The highs in a BPD relationship are intoxicating—filled with passion, romance, and intensity. Love is never boring; it's full of surprises, deep conversations, and intense emotions. A BPD partner may go out of their way to make their loved one feel wanted, special, and adored.

4. Fierce Loyalty & Protective Nature

If a BPD partner trusts and loves you, they are extremely loyal and protective. They may fight for the relationship harder than anyone else, refusing to give up. If they feel safe, they will stand by you no matter what.

5. Childlike Joy & Innocence

Many people with BPD have an inner child-like wonder—they love deeply, dream big, and feel joy intensely. They can be spontaneous, fun, and playful, making life feel vibrant. Their ability to experience emotions so fully means they appreciate small things in beautiful ways.

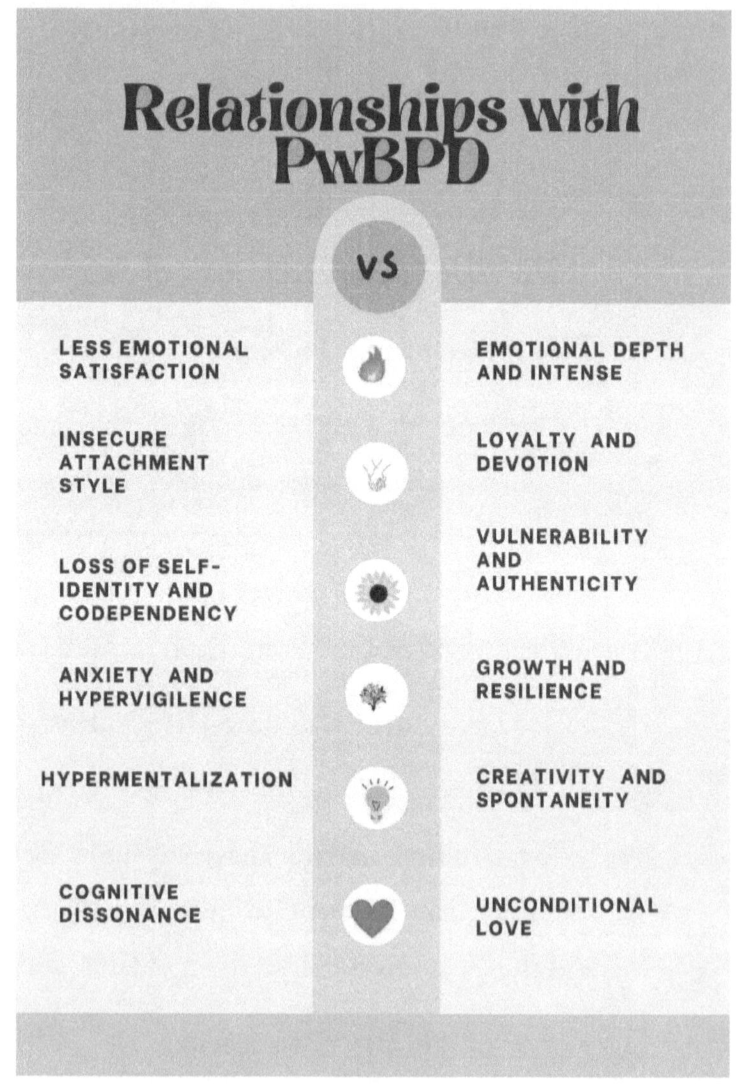

SETTING BOUNDARIES

Setting boundaries is a critical skill for individuals with Borderline Personality Disorder (BPD) and their loved ones. Boundaries help create a sense of safety, predictability, and respect in relationships, which are often areas of significant difficulty for those with BPD. Boundaries are the limits and rules we set for ourselves within relationships. They can be emotional, physical, or psychological and are essential for maintaining a sense of self and ensuring mutual respect and understanding in interactions with others.

COMMUNICATION STRATEGIES

Effective communication is a cornerstone of healthy relationships and emotional well-being. For individuals with Borderline Personality Disorder (BPD), communication can be particularly challenging due to intense emotions, fear of abandonment, and difficulties with self-identity. Communication involves the exchange of information, thoughts, and feelings between individuals. It encompasses verbal and non-verbal cues, active listening, and the ability to express oneself clearly and respectfully.

ACTIVE LISTENING

- **Paraphrasing**: Repeat back what the other person has said in your own words to ensure understanding.
- **Reflecting Feelings:** Acknowledge the emotions behind the words.
- **Asking Open-Ended Questions:** Encourage the other person to elaborate and share more.

NON-VERBAL COMMUNICATION

- **Eye Contact:** Maintain appropriate eye contact to show engagement.
- **Body Language:** Use open and relaxed body language to convey openness and receptivity.
- **Facial Expressions:** Ensure your facial expressions match your words to avoid mixed signals.

CHAPTER FIVE

PILLS AND POSSIBILITIES

While borderline personality disorder (BPD) was once considered largely resistant to psychotherapeutic interventions, the emergence of specialized treatment methods has fostered a more optimistic outlook. Currently, psychotherapy is recognized as the cornerstone of treatment for BPD, with medication only plays an adjunctive role.

When seeking professional medical help for Borderline Personality Disorder (BPD), it's essential to approach the process thoughtfully:

1. **Educate Yourself:** Understand the condition and the types of treatments available. This knowledge will empower you to make informed decisions.

2. **Consult Multiple Psychiatrists:** Visit 2-3 different psychiatrists to find one that best suits your needs or those of your loved one. Pay close attention to their attitude and approach to care.

3. **Evaluate Communication:** It's crucial that the psychiatrist clearly communicates the treatment plan and sets realistic expectations. BPD patients may develop a strong dependency on their doctor, desiring constant availability, which is not feasible. A good psychiatrist will address this in a compassionate and understandable way, helping to mitigate fears of abandonment and feelings of being unwanted.

4. **Understand the Treatment Plan:** Ask for a general outline of the treatment process. This helps in setting clear expectations and understanding the path forward. It's important to work with a professional who is well-versed in the latest advancements in psychiatric care, as some regions may have slower progress in this field.

5. **Beware of Discouraging Professionals:** Be cautious of psychiatrists who may downplay the severity of BPD or dismiss symptoms as mere pretenses, as this can be highly triggering and counterproductive. For instance, Jane, despite undergoing treatment for two years, was dismissed by a psychiatrist with 12 years of experience who claimed she was "just pretending." Such dismissiveness can exacerbate feelings of hopelessness and even lead to suicidal thoughts.

6. **Consistency is Key:** While it's important to find the right psychiatrist, frequently changing doctors can disrupt

the treatment process and delay progress. Careful consideration at the start can help ensure a more stable and effective therapeutic relationship.

By keeping these points in mind, you can better navigate the process of seeking professional help, ensuring that the chosen psychiatrist aligns well with the needs of the person with BPD.

"Remember, A Medical professional has their own limitations and can't be available all the time and this might be very frustrating because at this point you feel that only they can understand you better, which is very real to feel but they also can't let it disappear in a blink of eye. Healing need Trust, Time and Patience. For such scenarios, where you feel an urge to reach them out. Be prepared in advance – design your own personalized coping strategies. It can be a person, a task or an activity."

MEDICATION AND THERAPY OPTIONS

CLASSES OF MEDICATIONS FOR BORDERLINE PERSONALITY DISORDER (BPD)

Borderline Personality Disorder (BPD) is primarily managed through therapy. However, medication is often used to alleviate specific symptoms such as mood instability, impulsivity, depression, and anxiety. This chapter explores these medication classes, their potential benefits, and limitations.

1. ANTIDEPRESSANTS

Selective Serotonin Reuptake Inhibitors (SSRIs)

SSRIs are commonly prescribed to help manage the depressive and anxious symptoms of BPD. These medications increase serotonin levels in the brain, which can improve mood stability and emotional regulation. SSRIs are a class of antidepressants that work by increasing the levels of serotonin (a neurotransmitter associated with mood regulation) in the brain. They do this by blocking the reuptake of serotonin into neurons, making more serotonin available.

Common SSRIs: Fluoxetine (Prozac), Sertraline (Zoloft), Escitalopram (Lexapro)

Potential Benefits: Reduced depressive symptoms, improved emotional regulation, reduced impulsivity

Serotonin-Norepinephrine Reuptake Inhibitors (SNRIs)

SNRIs increase both serotonin and norepinephrine levels, potentially offering additional benefits for BPD patients with severe anxiety or fatigue. SNRIs are antidepressants that increase the levels of both serotonin and norepinephrine (a neurotransmitter involved in attention and energy) in the brain. They block the reuptake of both neurotransmitters.

Common SNRIs: Venlafaxine (Effexor), Duloxetine (Cymbalta)

Potential Benefits: May help with mood instability, anxiety, and emotional sensitivity

TCAs are an older class of antidepressants that increase the levels of serotonin and norepinephrine by blocking their reuptake.

2. MOOD STABILIZERS

Mood stabilizers are often prescribed to help with mood swings and impulsivity in BPD. While primarily used for bipolar disorder, they can be effective in reducing emotional instability.

Anticonvulsants (Used as Mood Stabilizers)

Some anticonvulsants help regulate mood and reduce impulsive behaviors.

Common Options: Lamotrigine (Lamictal), Valproate (Depakote), Topiramate (Topamax)

Potential Benefits: Reduction in mood swings, emotional reactivity, and impulsive aggression

3. ANTIPSYCHOTICS

Atypical antipsychotics are sometimes used for severe emotional dysregulation, paranoia, and dissociation. They affect dopamine and serotonin levels, helping to reduce distressing symptoms.

Common Options: Quetiapine (Seroquel), Olanzapine (Zyprexa), Risperidone (Risperdal), Aripiprazole.

Potential Benefits: May reduce emotional volatility, paranoia, dissociation, and aggression

4. ANTI-ANXIETY MEDICATIONS

Since anxiety is a major issue for many individuals with BPD, certain anti-anxiety medications may be prescribed.

Benzodiazepines (Used with Caution)

Benzodiazepines work quickly to reduce anxiety and agitation, but they come with risks of dependence and increased impulsivity.

Common Options: Alprazolam (Xanax), Clonazepam (Klonopin), Lorazepam (Ativan)

Potential Benefits: Immediate relief from anxiety and panic symptoms

Non-Benzodiazepine Alternatives

Buspirone (Buspar): A non-addictive anxiety medication that may be useful for generalized anxiety in BPD

Hydroxyzine (Vistaril): An antihistamine that provides short-term anxiety relief without dependency risks

OTHERS

Propranolol: A beta-blocker sometimes prescribed for severe anxiety and rage episodes.

LIMITATIONS OF MEDICATION FOR BPD

While medications can help manage symptoms, **they do not "cure" BPD.** They work best when combined with therapy, lifestyle changes, and coping strategies. Some medications may have side effects, require time to take effect, or lose effectiveness over time. Additionally, individuals with BPD may be more sensitive to side effects, making careful monitoring essential.

Key Considerations:

- Symptom-Specific Approach: Medications are chosen based on the individual's most distressing symptoms (e.g., mood swings, impulsivity, and anxiety).

- Combination with Therapy: Medications are most effective when used alongside evidence-based psychotherapy.

- Monitoring: Regular follow-ups are necessary to monitor side effects and adjust dosages.

TRANSFORMATIVE THERAPIES: NAVIGATING BPD TREATMENT

1. DIALECTICAL BEHAVIOR THERAPY (DBT)

DBT is designed to equip individuals with practical skills to navigate their daily lives more effectively. It focuses on enhancing emotional regulation, strengthening interpersonal relationships, increasing distress tolerance, and reducing harmful behaviors that negatively impact overall well-being. Developed by Psychologist **Marsha Linehan**, Dialectical Behavior Therapy (DBT) was originally created to address chronic suicidality in individuals with Borderline Personality Disorder (BPD). Over time, its application has expanded to support those struggling with various mental health conditions, including depression, self-harm, and substance use disorder. It was developed for specifically to address the emotional dysregulation and self-destructive behaviors common in BPD.

DBT promotes the formation of psychosocial and motivational skills. It employs evaluation protocols, individual and group therapy, telephone contact, and follow-up, with strategies based on a proposal for change within the context of the dialectical acceptance of reality. DBT provides an optimal therapeutic response in the reduction of self-injurious behaviors, suicidal thoughts and attempts.

Non-suicidal self-injury (NSSI) is characterized as the intentional and direct damage or modification of body tissue without a conscious intent to end one's life. This behavior is frequently linked to psychiatric conditions and is recognized as a core characteristic of Borderline Personality Disorder (BPD).

Individuals engage in self-harm for various reasons. A meta-analysis conducted by Klonsky identified seven primary functions of self-injury: **Affect regulation, Counteracting dissociation, self-punishment, influencing others, anti-suicide, establishing interpersonal boundaries,** and **sensation-seeking.** Dissociative symptoms, such as de-realization, depersonalization, and <u>psychogenic amnesia</u> (Memory loss defense mechanism against trauma or stress), are often reported as precursors to the urge to self-harm. Many individuals describe experiencing a sense of detachment or feeling as if they are operating on *"autopilot"* before engaging in self-injury. This behavior is often used as a means to reconnect with reality, experience physical sensations, and regain a sense of self.

TAKING OWNERSHIP OF RECOVERY

Recovery from Borderline Personality Disorder (BPD) or emotional dysregulation is a deeply personal journey that requires self-awareness, commitment, and active participation. Dialectical Behavior Therapy (DBT) emphasizes **self-sufficiency**—helping individuals take control of their emotions, behaviors, and choices rather than feeling powerless against them.

1. Tracking Emotions, Urges, and Behaviors

A crucial step in self-recovery is **monitoring patterns** in emotions, impulses, and reactions. This helps individuals recognize triggers, track progress, and develop healthier coping mechanisms.

Ways to Track Progress:

- Emotion Logs: Journaling daily feelings and their intensity.

- Urge Monitoring: Recording self-destructive urges and what triggered them.
- Behavior Analysis: Reflecting on responses to distressing situations and identifying patterns.
- Progress Journals: Documenting improvements and setbacks without self-judgment.

By understanding these patterns, individuals gain greater control over their responses rather than reacting impulsively.

2. Balancing Self-Acceptance and Change

DBT resolves the apparent contradiction between **self-acceptance** and **personal growth** by teaching that both **can coexist**. Accepting oneself as they are does not mean staying stuck—it means acknowledging one's struggles while working toward positive change.

Key Mindsets for Balance:

- Radical Acceptance: Accepting reality instead of resisting it, reducing suffering.
- Growth-Oriented Thinking: Focusing on progress, not perfection.
- Self-Compassion: Treating oneself with kindness rather than harsh criticism.

This balance helps individuals move forward without self-hatred or guilt, making change more sustainable.

3. Skills Training: Encouraging Positive Behaviors

Building a "life worth living" requires actively practicing skills that replace destructive habits with healthier ones.

By consistently applying these skills, individuals can break free from destructive cycles and build a stable, fulfilling future.

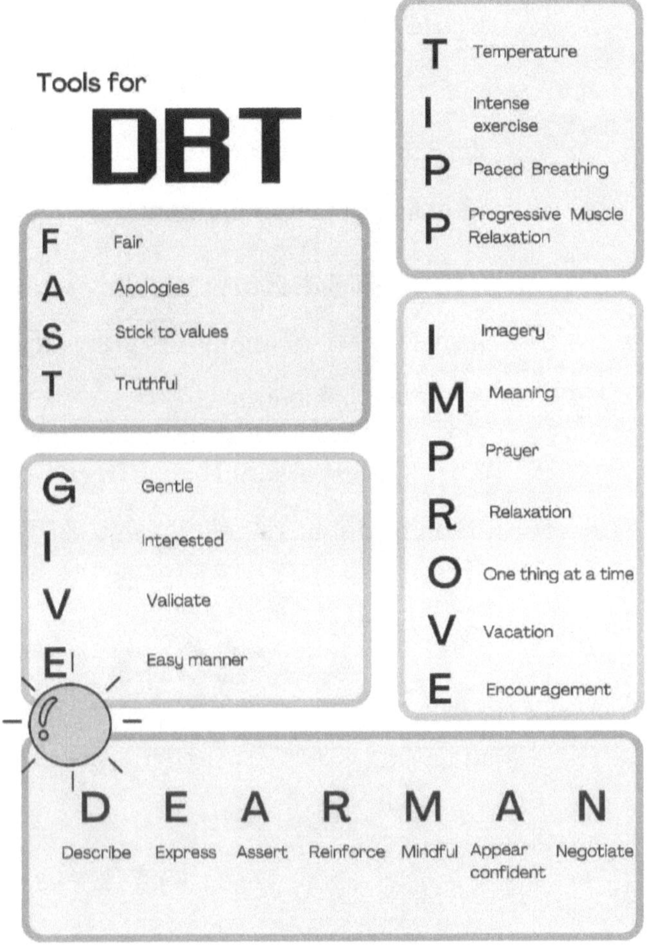

DBT combines individual therapy with group skills training. It focuses on four key areas:

1. Mindfulness: Learning to stay present in the moment and observe thoughts and feelings without judgment.

2. Emotion Regulation: Developing skills to manage and change intense emotions.

3. Distress Tolerance: Building the ability to tolerate and survive crises without resorting to self-harm or other destructive behaviors.

4. Interpersonal Effectiveness: Improving communication and relationship skills.

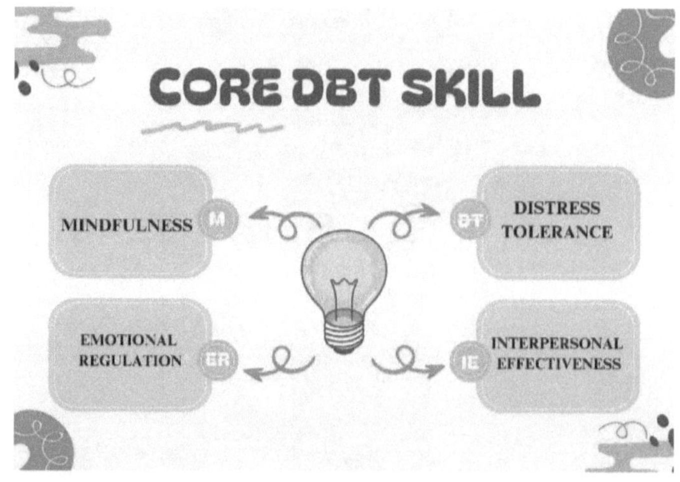

DBT provides practical tools for managing emotions and crises, making it particularly effective for reducing self-harm, suicidal behaviors, and emotional instability.

Dialectical Behavior Therapy (DBT) consists of four core modules designed to help individuals regulate emotions, build healthier relationships, tolerate distress, and develop mindfulness. Below is a detailed breakdown of each module and its techniques:

1. Mindfulness

Objective: Develop awareness and focus on the present moment without judgment.

Key Techniques:

Observing – Paying close attention to thoughts, emotions, and surroundings without reacting.

Describing – Putting experiences into words to create clarity and reduce impulsivity.

Participating – Fully engaging in the present moment instead of resisting or avoiding.

Non-Judgmental Stance – Accepting thoughts and emotions without labeling them as "good" or "bad."

One-Mindfully – Focusing on one task at a time instead of multitasking.

Effectiveness – Doing what works rather than getting stuck in what "should" be.

2. Distress Tolerance

Objective: Manage crises and tolerate distress without resorting to self-destructive behaviors.

Key Techniques:

TIPP (Temperature, Intense Exercise, Paced Breathing, Progressive Muscle Relaxation) – Rapidly changing body chemistry to reduce intense emotions.

Distract with ACCEPTS – Using healthy distractions:

A – Activities (hobbies, reading, music)

C – Contributing (helping others, volunteering)

C – Comparisons (thinking about past hardships overcome)

E – Emotions (watching a comedy or listening to uplifting music)

P – Pushing away (mentally setting aside distress temporarily)

T – Thoughts (engaging in puzzles, reading, or focusing on something else)

S – Sensations (using ice, a stress ball, or aromatherapy to shift focus)

Self-Soothe – Engaging the five senses to bring comfort (e.g., taking a warm bath, listening to calming music, using essential oils).

Radical Acceptance – Accepting reality fully instead of resisting it, reducing suffering.

IMPROVE the Moment –

I – Imagery (visualizing a safe place)

M – Meaning (finding purpose in suffering)

P – Prayer (seeking inner strength)

R – Relaxation (deep breathing, muscle relaxation)

O – One thing at a time (focusing on the present)

V – Vacation (taking a break, even mentally)

E – Encouragement (positive self-talk)

3. Emotion Regulation

Objective: Understand, manage, and change intense emotions to reduce emotional suffering.

Key Techniques:

PLEASE Skills – Managing emotional vulnerability through self-care:

PL – Physical health (exercise, sleep, and proper nutrition)

E – Eating balanced meals

A – Avoiding mood-altering substances

S – Sleeping enough

E – Engaging in exercise

Opposite Action – Acting opposite to an unhelpful emotional urge (e.g., if feeling sad and wanting to isolate, instead, engaging with loved ones).

Check the Facts – Examining whether emotions are based on facts or assumptions.

Building Positive Experiences – Engaging in enjoyable activities to create a fulfilling life.

Reducing Emotional Vulnerability – Practicing long-term emotional health strategies like gratitude, self-compassion, and routine.

4. Interpersonal Effectiveness

Objective: Improve communication, set boundaries, and maintain healthy relationships.

Key Techniques:

DEAR MAN (Assertive Communication for Getting Needs Met)

D – Describe the situation factually

E – Express feelings clearly

A – Assert needs confidently

R – Reinforce why it's beneficial for both

M – Be mindful (stay focused, don't get sidetracked)

A – Appear confident

N – Negotiate when needed

GIVE (Building & Maintaining Relationships)

G – Gentle (use a calm tone, avoid aggression)

I – Interested (show engagement in the other person's thoughts)

V – Validate (acknowledge their feelings)

E – Easy manner (use humor or kindness to keep things light)

FAST (Maintaining Self-Respect in Relationships)

F – Be Fair (to yourself and others)

A – Apologize less (don't over-apologize when unnecessary)

S – Stick to values (don't compromise on what matters)

T – Be Truthful (avoid exaggeration or dishonesty)

2. MENTALIZATION-BASED THERAPY (MBT)

Mentalizing-based approaches to understanding and treating borderline personality disorder emphasize three core capacities that play a central role in the development of this challenging condition: ***the ability to form secure attachment relationships***, ***the ability to mentalize*** (that is, to comprehend oneself and others in terms of intentional mental states), and ***the capacity for epistemic trust*** (the openness to viewing social information as potentially relevant and meaningful on a personal and broader level).

Complex trauma, often termed attachment trauma, developmental trauma, or type II trauma (in contrast to type I trauma, which involves single, isolated traumatic events), encompasses prolonged exposure to neglect and/or abuse, usually occurring within a caregiving or attachment relationship. For the child, this creates an unresolvable conflict, as the very individuals who are expected to provide safety and nurturing simultaneously become sources of fear, threat, anger, neglect, or harm.

Mentalization-Based Therapy (MBT) places a central emphasis on enhancing the capacity for mentalizing and epistemic trust, particularly within the context of attachment relationships. Its goal is to promote salutogenesis, or the development of health and well-being. As such, MBT is not solely focused on alleviating symptoms or improving relational functioning but also on fostering ongoing personal growth. A key aspect of MBT involves addressing the recurring interaction patterns that arise from vulnerabilities in mentalizing, especially within attachment dynamics. Given that the majority of individuals with borderline personality disorder have a history of complex trauma, trauma-focused work has always been an integral component of MBT for this population.

Mentalization-Based Therapy (MBT) Techniques

MBT focuses on improving self-awareness, reducing impulsivity, and enhancing interpersonal understanding. Below are key MBT techniques:

1. Increasing Self-Mentalization

Objective: Develop a clearer understanding of your own thoughts, emotions, and reactions.

Techniques:

Pause and Reflect: Before reacting impulsively, ask yourself:

What am I feeling right now?

Why am I feeling this way?

Is my interpretation of the situation accurate?

Naming Emotions: Instead of acting on feelings, identify them (e.g., "I feel abandoned" rather than "They hate me").

Checking for Emotional Shifts: Notice when emotions change suddenly and try to trace what triggered the shift.

Using a Mentalization Journal: Write about experiences, focusing on thoughts, emotions, and alternative explanations for events.

2. Enhancing Perspective-Taking

Objective: Understand that others have thoughts, emotions, and motivations separate from your own.

Techniques:

"What's going on in Their Mind?" Exercise:

Instead of assuming someone's intent, ask:

What might they be feeling?

What might be influencing their behavior?

Could there be another explanation for their actions?

Role Reversal: Imagine yourself in the other person's position—how would you see the situation differently?

Non-Judgmental Curiosity: Instead of assuming the worst about someone's intentions, stay curious and ask open-ended questions.

3. Improving Emotional Regulation through Mentalization

Objective: Avoid emotional dysregulation by reflecting before reacting.

Techniques:

The "Slow Down" Strategy: When emotions are high, take deep breaths and mentally step back before responding.

Reality Testing:

Are my thoughts facts or assumptions?

Am I predicting the future without evidence?

Have I misunderstood the situation?

Using a Mentalization "Anchor": Choose a trusted phrase (e.g., "I don't know everything about this situation yet") to ground yourself when feeling overwhelmed.

4. Strengthening Relationships with Mentalization

Objective: Build healthier interpersonal connections by reducing misunderstandings.

Techniques:

"Hold Multiple Perspectives": Accept that both your feelings and another person's feelings are valid, even if they seem conflicting.

Clarification Instead of Assumption: Ask the other person about their emotions rather than assuming their intent.

Repairing Misunderstandings: If a misinterpretation leads to conflict, revisit the conversation calmly and check for misunderstandings.

5. Developing a Mentalizing Stance

Objective: Cultivate a mindset that encourages ongoing self-reflection and curiosity about others.

Techniques:

"Not Knowing" Mindset: Accept that we don't always fully understand others' thoughts or our own, and that's okay.

Flexibility in Thinking: Be open to changing your perspective based on new information.

Seeking Constructive Feedback: Ask trusted individuals how they perceive your reactions and behaviors.

3. SCHEMA-FOCUSED THERAPY (SFT)

SFT integrates elements of cognitive-behavioral therapy (CBT), psychodynamic therapy, and attachment theory. It focuses on identifying and changing maladaptive schemas (deeply ingrained patterns of thinking and behavior).

The therapist helps the client identify early maladaptive schemas (e.g., abandonment, mistrust, defectiveness) that developed in childhood and continue to influence their behavior.

Through techniques like cognitive restructuring, imagery work, and role-playing, clients learn to challenge and change these schemas

Schemas are overarching and deeply ingrained patterns of thoughts, emotions, and behaviors that take shape during childhood or adolescence. They develop as a result of unmet core emotional needs—such as security, acceptance, and autonomy—during early life.

Common schemas include Abandonment, Defectiveness, Failure, and Emotional Deprivation. These patterns influence how individuals perceive themselves, others, and the world around them.

Early Maladaptive Schemas refer to dysfunctional core beliefs that create significant emotional distress. They stem from negative early-life experiences and tend to persist into adulthood, shaping behavior and emotional responses in unhealthy ways.

Schema modes represent temporary emotional states and coping mechanisms that individuals switch between when their schemas are triggered. Some common modes include:

- Child Modes (e.g., Vulnerable Child, Angry Child) – Reflect childhood emotional responses.

- Dysfunctional Coping Modes (e.g., Compliant Surrendered, Detached Protector) – Maladaptive behaviors developed to manage distress.

- Dysfunctional Parent Modes (e.g., Punitive Parent, Demanding Parent) – Internalized harsh or critical attitudes.

- Healthy Adult Mode – The balanced state therapy aims to cultivate, allowing for emotional regulation and healthier decision-making.

Coping Styles

To manage distressing schemas, individuals develop coping styles, though these often reinforce the problem rather than resolve it. The three main coping styles include:

Surrender – Accepting and reinforcing the schema, leading to behaviors that confirm the negative belief.

Avoidance – Steering clear of situations that might activate the schema, preventing emotional growth.

Overcompensation – Reacting in an exaggerated opposite manner to counteract the schema's influence.

The goal of Schema Therapy is to identify and modify these maladaptive patterns, promoting a shift toward healthier thought processes and emotional resilience.

4. TRANSFERENCE-FOCUSED PSYCHOTHERAPY (TFP)

TFP is a psychodynamic therapy that focuses on the relationship between the client and therapist to explore and understand distorted perceptions of self and others.

The therapist helps the client examine how they perceive and react to others, particularly in the context of the therapeutic relationship (transference).

By exploring these patterns, clients gain insight into their emotional struggles and learn to develop a more stable sense of self.

Key Therapeutic Techniques

Interpretation

The therapist helps the patient recognize and understand how their thoughts, feelings, and behaviors toward the therapist reflect past relational patterns and internalized experiences.

Example: *"It seems like you're expecting me to abandon you, similar to how you felt in your early relationships with your parents."*

Confrontation

The therapist gently highlights contradictions or inconsistencies in the patient's statements and behaviors to promote self-awareness and insight.

Example: *"You say our sessions don't matter to you, but you seem quite upset when we have to reschedule."*

Clarification

The therapist assists the patient in articulating their thoughts and emotions more clearly, especially when they feel vague or difficult to express.

Example: *"When you say you feel 'empty,' can you describe what that experience is like for you?"*

Working Through

Through repeated discussions and exploration of transference patterns, the therapist supports the patient in developing healthier ways of relating and processing emotions.

Establishing Boundaries

To ensure a safe and structured therapeutic environment, the therapist sets clear boundaries—an essential aspect of treatment for individuals with BPD.

5. ACCEPTANCE AND COMMITMENT THERAPY (ACT)

ACT is a mindfulness-based therapy that focuses on accepting difficult emotions and committing to actions aligned with one's values.

ACT teaches clients to observe their thoughts and feelings without judgment and to take action based on their core values, rather than being driven by emotions. Techniques include mindfulness exercises, cognitive defusion (distancing from thoughts), and values clarification.

6. SYSTEMS TRAINING FOR EMOTIONAL PREDICTABILITY AND PROBLEM SOLVING (STEPPS)

STEPPS is a group-based program that combines cognitive-behavioral techniques with skills training to help individuals with BPD manage their symptoms. STEPPS focuses on teaching emotional management, behavioral control, and problem-solving skills. It also involves family and friends in the treatment process, helping them understand BPD and support their loved one.

7. PSYCHODYNAMIC THERAPY

Psychodynamic therapy explores unconscious processes and past experiences to understand current behavior and emotional struggles. The therapist helps the client uncover unresolved conflicts and patterns from childhood that contribute to their symptoms. The focus is on gaining insight and developing a deeper understanding of oneself. Psychodynamic therapy can help individuals with BPD make sense of their emotions and behaviors, leading to lasting change.

8. GROUP THERAPY

Group therapy provides a supportive environment where individuals with BPD can share their experiences and learn from others. Group therapy can focus on specific skills (e.g., DBT skills) or provide a space for interpersonal learning and support. It helps individuals practice communication, empathy, and relationship skills in a safe setting.

CHAPTER SIX

COPING TOOLKIT

Managing Borderline Personality Disorder (BPD) requires a multifaceted approach, and developing personalized coping mechanisms can significantly enhance your healing journey.

PARENTS' PLAN FOR MITIGATING BORDERLINE PERSONALITY DISORDER (BPD) EPISODES

Parenting a child with Borderline Personality Disorder (BPD) can be overwhelming, especially when navigating their intense emotions, impulsive behaviors, and fear of abandonment. While individuals with BPD must develop their coping strategies, parents play a crucial role in mitigating episodes and creating a supportive environment. Understanding BPD Episodes

A BPD episode is a period of emotional dysregulation triggered by real or perceived stressors, often involving: Extreme mood swings , Intense fear of abandonment ,Self-harm or suicidal ideation ,Impulsivity (reckless spending, substance use, etc.) ,Explosive anger or withdrawal ,Dissociation or feelings of emptiness

1. <u>Building a Safe and Supportive Environment</u>

_A stable environment is the foundation of emotional regulation. Parents should:

- Maintain consistency: Avoid unpredictable behaviors, mixed signals, or sudden changes in routine.
- Reduce conflicts at home: A high-stress household exacerbates BPD symptoms. Keep discussions calm and avoid invalidating language.
- Encourage a non-judgmental space: Make sure your child feels heard without fear of being dismissed.

2. <u>Recognizing Early Warning Signs</u>

Identifying triggers before a full-blown episode can help parents intervene early. Signs to watch for:

- Increased irritability, withdrawal, or restlessness
- Talking about feeling abandoned, empty, or misunderstood
- Self-deprecating comments or drastic mood shifts
- Engaging in impulsive or reckless behaviors

3. <u>Responding to an Episode with De-escalation Techniques</u>

When an episode begins, a parent's reaction can either worsen or soothe it. Strategies include:

- Validating their emotions: Instead of dismissing their feelings, say, "I can see you're really hurting right now. I'm here for you."

- Speaking calmly and reassuringly: Avoid raising your voice or reacting emotionally.

- Setting boundaries without escalating the conflict: If they lash out, say, "I want to help, but I need us to talk without yelling."

- Providing a grounding activity: Encourage deep breathing, sensory objects, or a short walk to help regulate emotions.

4. <u>Teaching and Reinforcing Coping Mechanisms</u>

Parents can guide their child toward healthier emotional regulation by reinforcing coping skills like:

- Mindfulness and distress tolerance skills (e.g., breathing exercises, meditation)

- Journaling thoughts and emotions instead of acting impulsively

- Physical activity to release pent-up emotions

- Creative outlets (e.g., art, music) for self-expression

5. <u>Managing Crisis Situations (Self-Harm or Suicidal Ideation)</u>

If the episode escalates to self-harm or suicidal thoughts:

- Stay present: Do not leave them alone if they express suicidal intent.

- Remove immediate dangers: Keep sharp objects, medication, and alcohol away.

- Use crisis lines or emergency services if needed.

PARENTS PLAN FOR MITIGATING THE EPISODES

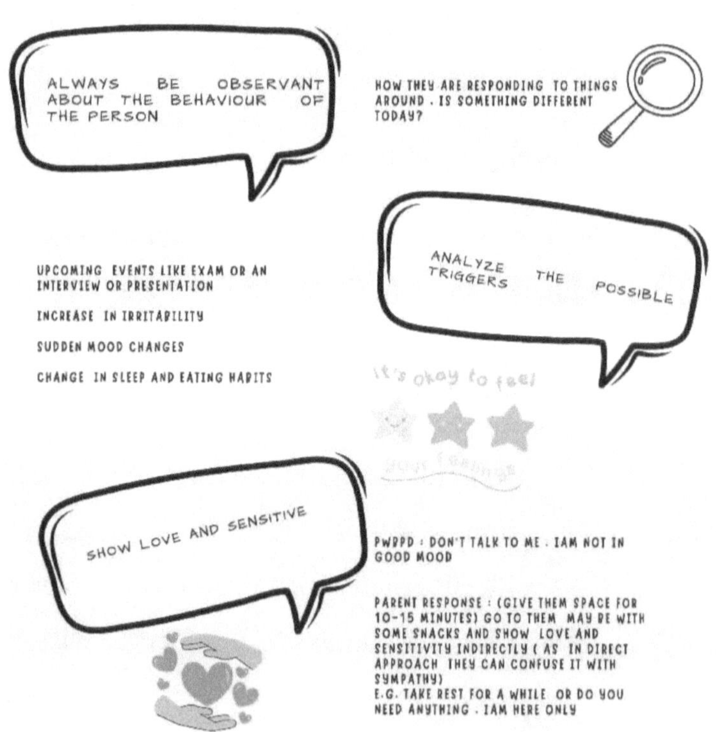

SUPPORTING A PARTNER WITH BPD DURING EPISODES

Being in a romantic relationship with someone who has Borderline Personality Disorder (BPD) comes with intense emotional highs and lows. Episodes of emotional dysregulation can strain even the strongest bonds, but a partner's response plays a crucial role in either escalating or soothing the situation.

UNDERSTANDING BPD EPISODES IN RELATIONSHIPS

Episodes are often triggered by: Fear of abandonment (real or perceived) ,Emotional invalidation,Conflict or rejection ,Sudden changes in plans ,Overwhelming stress or emotional pain

During an episode, a person with BPD may experience:

- Extreme mood swings (rage, sadness, despair)
- Impulsivity (reckless spending, self-harm, substance use)
- Splitting (seeing their partner as either "all good" or "all bad")
- Withdrawal or dissociation

- Accusations of betrayal or rejection

HOW PARTNERS CAN SUPPORT DURING AN EPISODE

1. <u>Recognizing the Signs Early</u>: Being aware of triggers and early warning signs can prevent escalation. Common indicators include:

- Increased anxiety, agitation, or hostility
- Reassurance-seeking (e.g., "Do you still love me?")
- Mood shifts after minor perceived slights
- Self-deprecating or self-harming thoughts

2. <u>Staying Calm and Validating Their Emotions</u>

Validation is key to de-escalating an episode. Instead of dismissing or arguing, say:

"I understand that you're feeling hurt right now. I want to be here for you."

"I can see this is really overwhelming. Let's take a deep breath together."

What NOT to say:

"You're overreacting." (Minimizing their feelings worsens distress.)

"I can't deal with this right now." (Reinforces fear of abandonment.)

"This is all in your head." (Invalidates their experience.)

3. <u>De-escalation Strategies</u>

When emotions run high:

- Remain present but non-reactive. Don't match their intensity.
- Use a soothing voice and body language. Stay open and non-threatening.
- Offer grounding techniques. Encourage deep breathing or sensory activities.
- Avoid power struggles. If they lash out, don't retaliate—set a calm boundary instead.

4. <u>Setting Healthy Boundaries</u>

Loving someone with BPD doesn't mean allowing harmful behavior. Boundaries should be firm yet compassionate:

> ***"I care about you, but I won't engage if we're yelling. Let's talk when we're calm."***

"I understand you're upset, but I need to step away for a moment. I'll be back when we can talk."

Boundaries should be clear and consistent, Protect both partners' emotional well-being , Not be punitive or used to control them

5. <u>Handling Self-Harm or Suicidal Thoughts</u>

If your partner expresses self-harm or suicidal thoughts:

- Stay present and listen. Do not dismiss their pain.

- Encourage professional help. Offer to help them access therapy.

- Ensure safety. If immediate danger exists, seek emergency assistance.

Reassure them without making false promises. Say, "You're not alone. We'll get through this together."

6. <u>Managing Your Own Well-Being</u>

Supporting a partner with BPD can be emotionally exhausting. To avoid burnout:

- Practice self-care. Prioritize your mental and emotional needs.

- Seek support. Therapy or support groups can provide guidance.

- Maintain independence. Have personal goals and social connections outside the relationship.

7. <u>Encouraging Long-Term Stability</u>

Beyond crisis moments, long-term stability comes from:

- Therapy (DBT, CBT) to develop coping skills
- Consistent communication and reassurance
- Practicing mindfulness and distress tolerance together
- Building trust through small, reliable actions

Loving someone with BPD requires patience, understanding, and strong boundaries. By validating emotions, de-escalating conflicts, and protecting your own well-being, you can foster a healthier, more stable relationship.

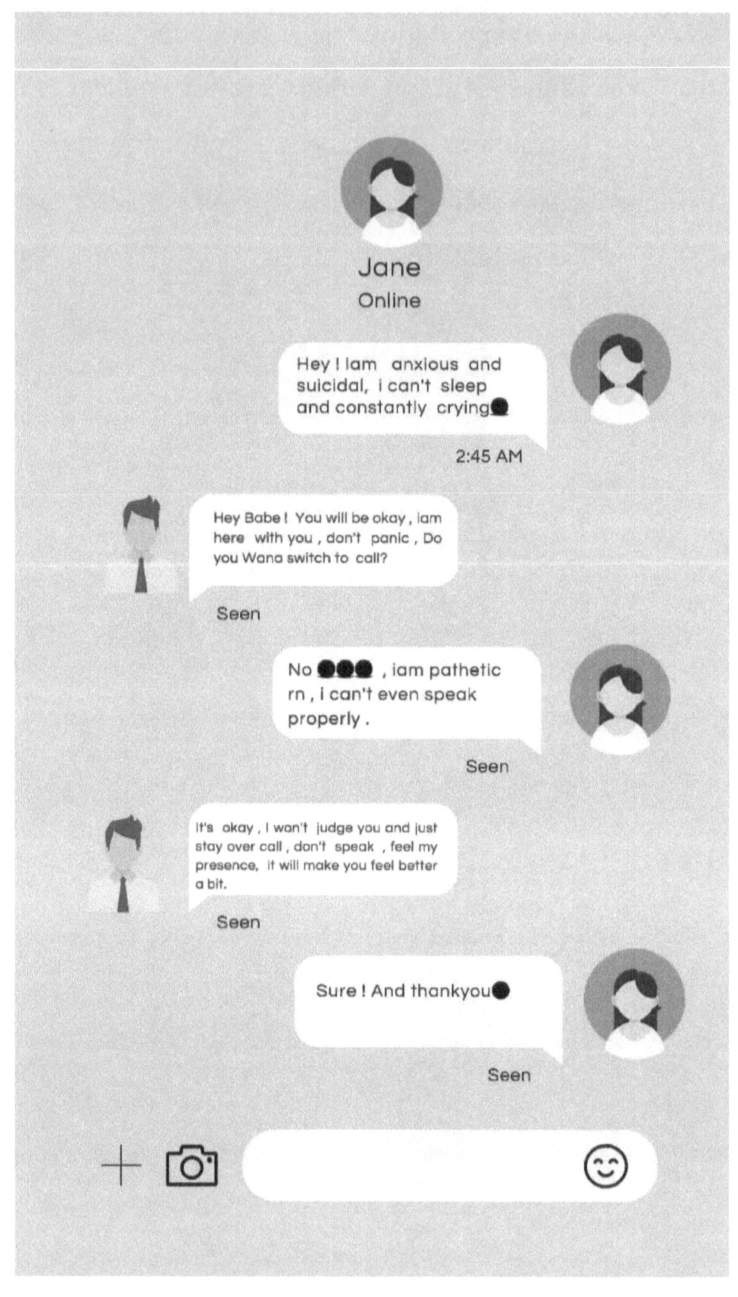

MITIGATING EMOTIONAL OUTBURSTS IN PUBLIC WITH BPD

For individuals with Borderline Personality Disorder (BPD), emotional outbursts can occur suddenly, triggered by stress, social anxiety, or perceived rejection. Experiencing these episodes in a public setting can be overwhelming, leading to embarrassment, guilt, or further dysregulation. Managing these situations requires a combination of self-awareness, grounding techniques, and pre-planned coping strategies

UNDERSTANDING PUBLIC TRIGGERS FOR BPD OUTBURSTS

Public settings can be overstimulating and unpredictable, making them challenging for emotional regulation. Common triggers include:

- Perceived rejection or criticism (e.g., a friend not responding warmly)
- Social overwhelm (e.g., loud crowds, unexpected interactions)
- Changes in plans (e.g., a canceled event, delayed transportation)
- Feeling ignored or invalidated
- Conflict in public with a partner, friend, or stranger

PREVENTIVE STRATEGIES BEFORE GOING OUT

Preparation is key to minimizing the risk of emotional outbursts in public.

1. Identifying High-Risk Situations

Before leaving home, reflect on potential triggers:

"Am I already feeling emotionally sensitive today?"

"Is this a high-stress environment for me?"

"Do I need an exit plan if I start feeling overwhelmed?"

2. Carrying a Coping Kit

A small emergency toolkit can provide comfort during distressing moments. Include:

- Noise-canceling earbuds or calming music
- A small object for grounding (stone, fidget toy)
- A written note with coping statements (e.g., "This feeling will pass.")
- A bottle of water to regulate breathing

3. Practicing Emotional Check-Ins

Before heading out, ask yourself:

"Where is my emotional state on a scale of 1-10?"

"If I start feeling overwhelmed, what's my first step?"

DE-ESCALATING AN OUTBURST IN PUBLIC

If emotions begin to spiral, these strategies can help regain control.

1. Recognizing the Early Warning Signs

Early signs of dysregulation include:Racing thoughts, rapid breathing, or heart pounding, Feeling hot or shaky ,Urge to lash out verbally or physically ,Sense of detachment from surroundings.

The sooner you recognize these signs, the easier it is to manage them.

2. Removing Yourself from the Stimulus

If possible, step away before the outburst escalates:

- Excuse yourself to a restroom, quiet corner, or an outdoor area.
- Use a pre-planned excuse like, "I need a moment to get some air."
- If alone, head to a less crowded space to regain composure.

3. Engaging in Grounding Techniques

Grounding can help shift focus away from overwhelming emotions:

- 5-4-3-2-1 Technique: Identify five things you can see, four you can touch, three you can hear, two you can smell, and one you can taste.

- Box breathing: Inhale for four seconds, hold for four seconds, exhale for four seconds, and repeat.
- Temperature shift: Hold a cold bottle of water or splash cool water on your face.

<u>4. Using a Safe, Repetitive Phrase</u>

Having a go-to statement can prevent impulsive reactions. Examples:

"I can handle this moment."

"I am safe. I can leave if I need to."

"This is temporary. I will feel better soon."

<u>5. Texting a Trusted Person</u>

If alone, reach out to someone for quick reassurance. A simple message like, "Feeling overwhelmed, need a distraction," can help ground you.

IF EMOTIONS ESCALATE DESPITE PREVENTIVE EFFORTS:

If with a friend/partner, signal your need for support. A phrase like "I need a moment" can let them know without drawing attention.

If crying or raising your voice, take slow breaths and lower your tone. This helps regain control and avoid unwanted attention.

If feeling confrontational, disengage and step away. Do not let the moment dictate your actions.

POST-EPISODE REFLECTION AND RECOVERY

After the episode, it's important to reflect and recover.

<u>1. Self-Compassion Over Shame</u>

Instead of self-criticism, remind yourself:

> *"I had a difficult moment, but I managed it."*

> *"I am not defined by one emotional outburst."*

> *"Next time, I will be even better prepared."*

<u>2. Identifying What Helped</u>

Ask yourself:

> *" What worked in calming me down?"*

> *"Did I notice any early warning signs?"*

> *"What can I do differently next time?"*

<u>3. Reassuring Those Around You (If Needed)</u>

If your episode affected someone else, a simple "I was feeling overwhelmed, but I'm okay now" can help ease concerns.

Managing emotional outbursts in public requires self-awareness, preparation, and quick regulation techniques. While avoiding triggers entirely isn't always possible, having a plan ensures that you can handle these moments with greater control and confidence.

MOOD CHARTING – A TECHNIQUE TO IDENTIFY THE POSSIBLE TRIGGERS AND SELF ANALYSIS

Tracking your triggers by writing them down can provide valuable insight into subconscious factors affecting your emotions. This process helps in identifying patterns, decoding underlying issues, and finding effective solutions. One useful technique is mood charting, where you rate your mood on a scale from 1 to 10—1 being the lowest and 10 the highest. By consistently monitoring these patterns, you can develop personalized coping strategies tailored to your emotional fluctuations.

MOOD CHARTING

Date:15.Oct.2023

Time : 08:35 PM

Mood Rating

4/10

Iam feeling pathetic right now, day was okay but now in the evening iam experiencing irritating mood, anxiety kicked in all of sudden and now i feel discouraged about life, i went to the work, everything was okay there, i came home by walking, ate well after coming back home. Zack called and was talking about one of his collegue having bad time with mental health and had divorce due to this and now juggling with relationships and commitments. Then i started listening music after that call and since then my mood became cranky maybe I don't feel like talking to anyone and a feeling of abandonment kicking in because i feel that i could be like her and i will be miserable in future

THINGS TO CONSIDER WHILE FORMULATING PERSONALIZED COPING STRATIEGIES

1. Reduce Screen Time

Excessive screen time can lead to irritability, emotional outbursts, and insomnia—symptoms that can be particularly challenging for individuals with BPD. Here's how you can gradually decrease screen usage:

- *Limit Social Media Exposure*: Social media often showcases curated and glamorous lives, which can trigger feelings of inadequacy or comparison. Reducing your presence on these platforms can help you focus on your reality without external triggers.

- *Replace Screen Time with Other Activities:* Redirect the time spent on devices toward fulfilling hobbies, such as cooking, baking, cleaning, or gardening. Start small and allow yourself to enjoy these activities gradually.

2. Find Joy in Simple, Repetitive Activities

Engaging in repetitive tasks can be calming and satisfying. These activities help distract you from overthinking and reduce hypermentalization.

These activities can be helpful and you can find such more as per your interests

- *Doodling or Mandala Art*: These require focus and can break the cycle of negative thought patterns.
- *Crocheting or Knitting*: Crafting with your hands can be both therapeutic and rewarding.

3. Increase active hours

Inactivity might feel comforting in the short term, but it often leads to feelings of low self-esteem, negativity, and overthinking.

Incorporate physical activities into your day and gradually increase the duration

- *Walking*: A simple walk can increase brain

activity, improve mood, and maintain healthy brain chemical levels.

- *Cycling or Working Out*: Exercise promotes endorphin release, which can elevate your mood and provide a sense of accomplishment.

4. Build Responsibility through Pet Care

Caring for a pet can generate a sense of responsibility and inner motivation. Feeding, grooming, and playing with a pet can help create a structured daily routine and encourage physical activity.

5. Engage with Music

Listening to a song repeatedly can create a sense of comfort, especially when silence feels overwhelming. Designate a song as your "stress song" and use it to drown out intrusive inner voices or negative thoughts.

6. Explore New Skills and Hobbies

- Learning something new can boost your confidence and break the cycle of inactivity. Try Skill-Based Hobbies: Writing, painting, or even baking.
- Self-Employment or Small Projects: Start small—this can gradually build your confidence and give you a sense of purpose.

7. Nourish Your Body

A healthy diet is crucial for emotional and physical well-being. Consider incorporating nutrient-rich foods and avoiding substances like alcohol or drugs, as they can exacerbate symptoms.

8. Travelling to find yourself can be game changer

Traveling and staying in hostels can be a great way for people with BPD to socialize in a low-pressure environment, as interactions are temporary and free from long-term expectations. It provides distraction from emotional turmoil, helps build self-sufficiency, and allows for practicing social skills without the fear of deep rejection. Engaging with like-minded travelers fosters connection while maintaining personal space, reducing the intensity of emotional attachments. While challenges like fear of abandonment or impulsivity may arise, mindful self-regulation can make the experience a valuable opportunity for growth, independence, and emotional resilience.

9. Validate and Regulate Your Emotions

Emotional vulnerability is a hallmark of BPD. Develop strategies to manage these moments effectively:

- *Safe Spaces*: When feeling emotionally overwhelmed, retreat to a safe space or be with trusted individuals who can support you without judgment.
- *Limit Impulsive Behaviors*: When you feel the urge to act impulsively, such as oversharing, gently remove yourself from the situation.

10. Healthy Alternatives for Self-Harm

If you struggle with self-harm, consider alternatives that allow you to experience a physical sensation without causing harm:

- *Ice Cubes*: Hold ice cubes to feel a sensation that

grounds you without injury.

- *Rubber Bands*: Snap a rubber band on your wrist as a distraction during intense emotional moments.

11. Set Boundaries for Impulsive Behavior

Hyper sexuality or low sexual interest are common in BPD. Create clear boundaries for yourself and Set Ground Rules: Establish limits to guide your actions during moments of impulsivity .Create Healthy Outlets try to channel your energy into productive activities.

12. Stay Hopeful and Consistent

Healing is not about finding extraordinary solutions but about consistently practicing simple, effective strategies. Believe in your ability to adapt and grow.

- *Create Personalized Coping Mechanisms*: Find what works best for you through trial and error.
- *Never Lose Hope*: Adopt the mindset that a solution always exists—you just need to keep searching for it, it might take long but it's always there and it's never too late!

CHAPTER SEVEN
STILL A LONG TURBULENT JOURNEY

There will be days when the emotional storms feel overwhelming, when relationships are strained, and when the weight of the world seems too much to bear. But **even in the midst of this turbulence, there is hope**. Recovery is not a straight path—it's a winding road with ups and downs, and that's okay.

BPD isn't something that simply disappears—it's a condition you learn to navigate by reshaping the way you live. Life won't follow a straight, predictable path; it's a series of highs and lows. Each day brings new challenges, but with time, you develop the skills to manage them more effectively. It's not always smooth, but it is possible.

1. Embrace the Progress, No Matter How Small

- <u>Celebrate the Wins</u> - Recovery is *not about perfection; it's about progress*. Celebrate the small victories—whether it's using a coping skill during a moment of distress, reaching out for support, or simply getting out of bed on a hard day. These moments matter.

- <u>Track Your Growth-</u> Keep a journal or a list of the skills you've learned, the challenges you've overcome, and the ways you've grown. Reflecting on how far you've come can be a powerful reminder of your strength.

2. Cultivate Self-Compassion

- <u>Be Kind to yourself</u> - Living with BPD can be exhausting, and it's easy to fall into self-criticism. Instead, practice self-compassion.

Remind yourself that you are doing the best you can with the tools you have. Treat yourself with the same kindness you would offer a friend.

- <u>Let Go of Shame</u> - Shame often accompanies BPD, but it doesn't define you. You are not your diagnosis, and you are not your mistakes. Let go of the shame and focus on who you are becoming.

3. Build a Support System

- <u>Lean on Others</u> - You don't have to navigate this journey alone. Surround yourself with people who understand and support you—whether it's friends, family, a therapist, or a support group. Connection is a powerful antidote to feelings of isolation.

- <u>Communicate Your Needs</u> - Let your loved ones know how they can support you. Whether it's a listening ear, a distraction, or simply their presence, clear communication can strengthen your relationships.

4. Focus on What You Can Control

- <u>Accept the Unpredictable</u> - Life with BPD can feel chaotic, but there are always aspects of your life that you can control. Focus on your reactions, your choices, and the steps you can take to care for yourself.

- <u>Practice Mindfulness</u> - Mindfulness can help you stay grounded in the present moment, even when emotions feel overwhelming. It's not about eliminating the turbulence but learning to ride the waves.

5. Find Meaning and Purpose

- <u>Discover Your Passions</u> - What brings you joy? Whether it's art, music, writing, helping others, or spending time in nature, engaging in activities that light you up can provide a sense of purpose.

- <u>Set Meaningful Goals</u> - Recovery is not just about managing symptoms—it's about building a life worth living. Set goals that align with your values and dreams, no matter how big or small.

6. Remember: Recovery is Possible

- <u>Hold onto Hope </u>- Research shows that many people with BPD experience significant improvement over time, especially with the right treatment and support. Recovery is not a myth—it's a reality for countless individuals.

- <u>You Are Not Alone</u> - There is a community of people who understand what you're going through. Reach out, share your story, and draw strength from others who have walked a similar path.

To

    My BPD Warrior

Life have been harsh and unfair to you all. The pain which is now impossible to bear is not leaving. The wounds are always fresh and burning everyday. The life seems in dark. Every other hour seems ending everything and you can't trust anyone though you badly want to. I can feel your pain, we can feel your pain And those who can't don't have the ability to, so it better to forgive them. You are the most beautiful soul. Have faith in yourself, even if they failed to. Choose yourself, if they didn't and this doesn't make you a bad person at all. Its just they want something else. Just learn this art of accepting things, forgiving them and yourself and letting go. Consider yourself more evolved than anyone. You can feel too much in this heartless world. Start turning your pain into your strength and wear it like jewel. Show yourself and to the world that even you passed this. Shout out loud to those who doubted you and your capabilities. Shake their confidence the way they mocked yours. Now, Its all about YOU, their will be bad days still but that don't make the entire canvas of life dark.

                                Kunjan Sharma

REFERENCES

American Psychiatric Association. (2022). *Diagnostic and statistical manual of mental disorders* **(5th ed., text rev.)**

Bouchard S, Sabourin S, Lussier Y, Villeneuve E. Relationship quality and stability in couples when one partner suffers from borderline personality disorder. Journal of marital and family therapy. 2009 Oct;35(4):446-55.

Gratz KL, Kiel EJ, Mann AJ, Tull MT. The prospective relation between borderline personality disorder symptoms and suicide risk: The mediating roles of emotion regulation difficulties and perceived burdensomeness. Journal of affective disorders. 2022 Sep 15;313:186-95.

Gunderson, J. G., & Links, P. (Collaborator). (2014). *Handbook of good psychiatric management for borderline personality disorder.* American Psychiatric Publishing, Inc.

Mendez-Miller M, Naccarato J, Radico JA. Borderline personality disorder. American family physician. 2022 Feb;105(2):156-61.

Navarro-Gómez S, Frías Á, Palma C. Romantic relationships of people with borderline personality: A narrative review. Psychopathology. 2017 May 19;50(3):175-87.

Pohl S, Steuwe C, Mainz V, Driessen M, Beblo T. Borderline personality disorder and childhood trauma: Exploring the buffering role of self-compassion and self-esteem. Journal of clinical psychology. 2021 Mar;77(3):837-45.

Smits ML, Luyten P, Feenstra DJ, Bales DL, Kamphuis JH, Dekker JJ, Verheul R, Busschbach JJ. Trauma and outcomes of mentalization-based therapy for individuals with borderline personality disorder. American journal of psychotherapy. 2022 Jan 1;75(1):12-20.